Emeril Lagasse
French Doors
AIR FRYER
OVEN COOKBOOK

Baiyurbora Duspiveriy

2000 Days Easy, Tasty & Quick Dual Zone Air Fryer Oven Recipes Book for Beginners to Fry, Grill, etc. | Stress-Free 30-Day Meal Plan

TABLE OF CONTENTS

INTRODUCTION

Welcome to the world of fast, flavorful, and healthy cooking with the Emeril Lagasse French Doors Air Fryer Oven. This groundbreaking kitchen appliance has taken the home cooking world by storm, offering the versatility and convenience that modern households need. With its unique design and multiple cooking functions, this air fryer oven is not just another gadget—it's an all-in-one cooking solution that will elevate your culinary game.

This cookbook is your guide to unlocking the full potential of the Emeril Lagasse French Doors Air Fryer Oven. Whether you're a seasoned home cook or new to the kitchen, this book will help you explore the endless possibilities of this appliance, allowing you to create delicious, healthy meals in less time than traditional methods.

The Evolution of Home Cooking

Home cooking has always been at the heart of family life, but the way we cook has evolved dramatically over the years. In the past, preparing meals often required a variety of appliances—ovens, stovetops, deep fryers, toasters, and more. Not only did this create a cluttered kitchen, but it also meant that cooking could be a time-consuming and labor-intensive process. Today, with the demands of busy lifestyles, the need for efficient, versatile, and healthier cooking methods has never been more important.

That's where the Emeril Lagasse French Doors Air Fryer Oven comes in. It represents the next step in the evolution of home cooking, combining the functionality of multiple kitchen appliances into one compact unit. This air fryer oven simplifies meal preparation while allowing you to create dishes that are just as delicious as those made using traditional methods. And with the added benefit of cooking with less oil and in less time, this appliance makes it easier than ever to maintain a healthy lifestyle without sacrificing flavor.

The French Doors Design: A New Level of Convenience

One of the standout features of the Emeril Lagasse French Doors Air Fryer Oven is its innovative French doors design. Unlike traditional air fryers or toaster ovens that require you to open a single door, this appliance features two doors that open outward. This design has several benefits:

♦ **Easy access:** The French doors make it easier to insert and remove food from the oven without losing heat, which helps maintain the cooking temperature for more consistent results.

♦ **Safety and convenience:** With the ability to open just one door or both, the French doors reduce the risk of accidentally burning yourself, especially when handling large or hot dishes.

♦ **Better visibility:** The large, clear glass doors allow you to keep an eye on your food as it cooks without the need to open the oven and release heat.

This simple yet innovative design sets the Emeril Lagasse French Doors Air Fryer Oven apart from other appliances, offering a more convenient and efficient cooking experience.

Multiple Cooking Functions for Every Need

One of the reasons the Emeril Lagasse French Doors Air Fryer Oven stands out is its impressive range of cooking functions. Whether you want to air fry, bake, roast, or dehydrate, this appliance has you covered. It's not just an air fryer—it's an all-in-one cooking machine designed to handle almost any type of meal you can think of.

Here's a closer look at some of its key functions:

♦ **Air frying:** Get the crispy texture of fried foods with little to no oil, reducing calories and unhealthy fats.

♦ **Rotisserie:** Cook a whole chicken or roast to perfection with the included rotisserie function, giving you restaurant-quality results at home.

♦ **Baking:** Use the oven to bake cakes, cookies, bread, and more, with even heat distribution for consistent results.

♦ **Dehydrating:** Make your own dried fruits, vegetables, or jerky using the dehydrate function, perfect for healthy snacks.

♦ Broiling and roasting: Get a perfectly charred finish on meats and vegetables, or slow roast your favorite cuts of meat for tender, juicy results.

This multifunctionality means that you can reduce the number of appliances in your kitchen, save space, and still enjoy a wide variety of cooking techniques.

The Science Behind Air Frying

Air frying has revolutionized how we think about cooking, particularly when it comes to preparing fried foods in a healthier way. Traditional frying methods rely on submerging food in oil, which adds excess fat and calories to your meals. In contrast, air frying uses hot air circulation to cook food evenly while creating a crispy exterior without the need for large amounts of oil.

The Emeril Lagasse French Doors Air Fryer Oven uses rapid air technology to cook food from all sides, mimicking the effects of deep frying but with up to 70% less fat. The result is food that's crunchy on the outside, tender on the inside, and significantly healthier than its traditionally fried counterparts.

The science behind air frying is simple but effective. The hot air in the oven circulates around the food, cooking it evenly while the high temperatures ensure that moisture is retained, preventing dryness. This method not only makes food healthier but also cooks it faster than conventional methods, allowing you to prepare meals in a fraction of the time.

Sustainable and Energy-Efficient Cooking

In addition to being healthier, the Emeril Lagasse French Doors Air Fryer Oven is also a more sustainable choice for your kitchen. Traditional ovens and stovetops use more energy and often require longer cooking times. In contrast, the air fryer oven uses convection heating, which is far more energy-efficient and reduces overall cooking time. This not only helps save on electricity but also contributes to a smaller carbon footprint.

For households that are trying to reduce their energy consumption or make more environmentally conscious decisions, this appliance is an excellent choice. Its compact size and energy-efficient design make it ideal for cooking small to medium-sized meals without wasting excess energy on heating a full-sized oven.

Cooking with Confidence: Precision and Control

Another feature that makes the Emeril Lagasse French Doors Air Fryer Oven stand out is its precision control. Whether you're cooking a delicate pastry or roasting a large cut of meat, the oven's temperature and time settings give you full control over the cooking process. This precision ensures that your food is cooked perfectly every time, whether you're air frying, baking, or using the rotisserie function.

Many recipes can be intimidating, especially if they require exact timing or temperatures, but the preset cooking functions and intuitive controls on the Emeril Lagasse French Doors Air Fryer Oven remove the guesswork. This allows you to cook with confidence, knowing that the appliance will deliver consistent results.

Elevate Your Culinary Experience

Cooking is more than just a necessity—it's an art form, a way to express creativity, and an opportunity to bring people together. The Emeril Lagasse French Doors Air Fryer Oven opens the door to new culinary possibilities, allowing you to experiment with flavors, textures, and techniques that were previously time-consuming or difficult to achieve.

Whether you're preparing a quick weeknight dinner, hosting a family gathering, or experimenting with gourmet recipes, this air fryer oven provides the tools you need to create memorable meals with ease. With its combination of innovation, efficiency, and versatility, the Emeril Lagasse French Doors Air Fryer Oven isn't just a kitchen appliance—it's a gateway to a more enjoyable, stress-free cooking experience.

Conclusion

The Emeril Lagasse French Doors Air Fryer Oven is transforming the way we cook, offering a healthier, faster, and more convenient way to prepare meals without compromising on taste or quality. As you explore the recipes in this cookbook, you'll discover the full potential of this remarkable appliance. Whether you're air frying for the first time or looking to expand your repertoire, this book will guide you toward mastering the art of cooking with the Emeril Lagasse French Doors Air Fryer Oven. Happy cooking!

30-Day Meal Plan

DAYS	BREAKFAST	LUNCH	DINNER	SNACK/DESSERT
1	Ricotta Spinach Frittata 10	Air-Fried Chicken Pepper Fajitas 26	Herb-Roasted Rosemary Pork Belly 33	Air Fryer Cinnamon Apple Fritters 70
2	Cinnamon Yogurt Pancake Bites 12	Avocado Turkey Sliders 24	Crispy Cheese-Crusted Sirloin Chops 37	Cinnamon Plum Pie Cups 67
3	Air-Fried Cinnamon French Toast 10	Roasted Chicken and Carrot Salad 26	Garlic-Spiced Skirt Steak 32	Air Fryer Chocolate Glazed Eclairs 70
4	Zucchini Chickpea Cheese Bites 10	Cheesy Italian Chicken Fillets 23	Mustard Garlic Shredded Beef Brisket 39	Cinnamon Apple Spice Cake 69
5	Spinach Egg Cream Cheese Cups 14	Garlic Butter Chicken Breasts 22	Blue Cheese Pork Tenderloin with Mushrooms 30	Coconut Blueberry Fritters 68
6	Herbed Tomato Mozzarella Frittata 9	Spicy Hot Chicken Thighs 24	T-bone Steak Salad with Tomato and Lime 32	Cocoa Spice Cupcakes 69
7	Feta Spinach Mini Tartlets 12	Sun-Dried Tomato and Mozzarella Stuffed Chicken 23	Cuban Pork and Cheese Sandwich 39	Air Fryer Raisin Butter Scones 68
8	Spiced Potato Bites 9	Herbed Pork Chops with Bell Peppers 32	Sesame Garlic Beef Tenderloin 32	Pumpkin Spice Honey Cake 69
9	Roasted Chickpea Spinach Bowl 8	Garlic-Infused Pork Ribs 31	Crispy Panko-Crusted Salmon Strips 41	Crispy Paprika Potato Chips 49
10	Herbed Air-Fried Potato Bites 11	Beef and Broccoli Patties 31	Herb-Infused Butter Sea Bass 42	Cinnamon Pear Pancake Bake 67
11	Cheesy Corn Fritters 9	Espresso-Rubbed Sirloin Roast 30	Parmesan-Crusted Monkfish Fillets 42	Cinnamon Apple Cream Cheese Rolls 19
12	Mushroom Swiss Frittata Delight 12	Spicy Beef Burger Buns 30	Spicy Lemon Prawns with Garlic 43	Sweet and Savory Chicken Wings 49
13	Air-Fried Cinnamon Butter Toast 9	Honey Soy Duck Fillet 23	Smoky Paprika Pork Loin Chops 33	Herbed Sweet Potato Chips 51
14	Spicy Barley Walnut Croquettes 8	Greek-Seasoned Chicken Fillets 24	Garlic-Seasoned Sea Bass 43	Spicy Mustard Chicken Wings 50
15	Walnut Quinoa Bean Sausages 13	Rotisserie Lemon Oregano Chicken 24	Paprika and Parsley Squid Tubes 44	Tangy Vinegar Chicken Drumettes 51
16	Crispy Broccoli Seed Salad 11	Lemon Cream Chicken Salad 25	Herbed Butter Mahi-Mahi Fillets 44	Cumin-Seasoned Wax Beans 50

DAYS	BREAKFAST	LUNCH	DINNER	SNACK/DESSERT
17	Lemon Garlic Cauliflower Salad 10	Five-Spice Sesame Chicken Drumsticks 25	Savory Sausage-Stuffed Squid 46	Spicy Chili Cauliflower Bites 49
18	Spicy Air-Fried Chickpeas 10	Crispy Turkey Schnitzel 22	Lime-Glazed Ham with Spices 31	Savory Glazed Pork Ribs 53
19	Sesame Tofu Pepper Bowl 11	Cheddar Chicken Muffin Melts 25	Citrus-Marinated Cuban Pork Tenderloin 31	Crispy Air-Fried Mixed Nuts 50
20	Mushroom Bulgur Fritters 13	Parmesan Garlic Chicken Wings 23	Crispy Coconut Shrimp 43	Cinnamon Egg Donuts 68
21	Parmesan Pork and Turkey Meatballs 14	Smoked Sausage with Crispy Onion Rings 32	Garlic Mayo Air Fryer Green Beans 62	Garlic Butter Air Fryer Potatoes 55
22	Crispy Buckwheat Parmesan Bites 12	Smoky Butter Chicken Cutlets 25	Spiced Air Fryer Cauliflower Bites 61	Parmesan-Dill Air Fryer Broccoli 55
23	Air-Fried Sausage Swiss Roll-Ups 12	Spicy Cayenne Chicken Legs 25	Herb-Crusted Air Fryer Potatoes with Thyme 62	Spiced Peppercorn Potato Chips 51
24	Cinnamon Apple Oat Muffins 20	Red Wine Marinated Turkey Wings 26	Turmeric-Spiced Air Fryer Cauliflower 61	Spicy Chili Air Fryer Potatoes 56
25	Honey Almond Baked Oatmeal 19	Marinated Rice Wine Chicken Breasts 22	Spicy Bacon and Tomato Sandwich 33	Spicy Air Fryer Bell Peppers 57
26	Buttermilk Raisin Scones 18	Herbed Breaded Chicken Schnitzel 23	Herbed Air Fryer Polenta with Marinara 62	Spicy Chile Pork Ribs 53
27	Herbed Scallion Rice Pilaf 19	Creamy Corn Butter Fritters 17	Lentil-Stuffed Air Fryer Eggplant 65	Spicy Paprika Tortilla Chips 53
28	Pumpkin Spice Cranberry Granola 17	Herbed Lemon Salmon Fillets 43	Herb-Crusted Pork Burgers 33	Cinnamon-Spiced Apple Chips 51
29	Honey Coconut Prune Bread Pudding 17	Mozzarella Mac and Cheese Bake 16	Butter-Basted Coulotte Roast 33	Maple Glazed Pancetta-Wrapped Shrimp 51
30	Tropical Pineapple Coconut Oatmeal 18	Spicy Mackerel Patties on English Muffins 41	Rosemary-Infused Swordfish Steaks 46	Herbed Air-Fried Potato Chips 50

Chapter 1

Breakfasts

Chapter 1 Breakfasts

Spicy Barley Walnut Croquettes

Prep time: 5 minutes | Cook time: 15 minutes | Serves 4

- 1½ cups cooked barley
- 2 large eggs, beaten
- 1 cup bread crumbs
- Kosher salt and cayenne pepper, to taste
- 1 teaspoon red chili powder
- 2 ounces (57 g) ground walnuts
- 2 tablespoons olive oil

1. Begin by setting the air fryer to 380°F (193°C) to preheat.2. In a mixing bowl, thoroughly blend all the ingredients until fully incorporated, then shape the mixture into small balls and place them into the crisper tray.3. Position the crisper tray in the air fryer, choose the Air Fry setting, and cook the balls for approximately 15 minutes or until they are fully cooked, making sure to shake the tray halfway through to ensure even cooking.

Crispy Parmesan Potato Croquettes

Prep time: 10 minutes | Cook time: 14 minutes | Serves 4

- ½ cup all-purpose flour
- ¾ pound (340 g) potatoes, peeled and grated
- 2 eggs, whisked
- 2 tablespoons butter
- 2 ounces (57 g) Parmesan cheese, grated
- 2 ounces (57 g) bread crumbs
- 2 tablespoons olive oil
- 1 teaspoon paprika
- Kosher salt and freshly ground black pepper, to taste

1. Preheat the air fryer to 400°F (205°C). 2. Combine all the ingredients in a bowl and form the mixture into small, bite-sized balls. Lightly oil the crisper tray and arrange the balls on it. 3. Insert the crisper tray into the air fryer. Choose the Air Fry function and cook the croquettes for around 14 minutes, giving the tray a shake halfway through to ensure even cooking.

Roasted Chickpea Spinach Bowl

Prep time: 6 minutes | Cook time: 28 minutes | Serves 3

- 8 ounces (227 g) chickpeas, drained and rinsed
- 2 tablespoons olive oil
- Sea salt and ground black pepper, to taste
- 1 teaspoon paprika
- 2 bell peppers, seeded and halved
- 1 small onion, thinly sliced
- 2 cups baby spinach
- 2 lemon wedges

1. Start by preheating the air fryer to 390°F (199°C). 2. Toss the chickpeas with the olive oil, salt, black pepper, and paprika in the crisper tray. 3. Place the crisper tray in the corresponding position in the air fryer. Select Air Fry and cook the chickpeas for about 13 minutes, tossing the crisper tray a couple of times; reserve. 4. Increase the temperature to 400°F (205°C). Place the crisper tray in the corresponding position in the air fryer. Select Air Fry and cook the peppers for about 15 minutes, shaking the crisper tray halfway through the cooking time. 5. Arrange the bowl with the roasted chickpeas, peppers, and the other ingredients.

Cheesy Miso Potato Sticks

Prep time: 6 minutes | Cook time: 14 minutes | Serves 4

- 1 cup mashed boiled potato
- 1 cup grated Cheddar cheese
- 1 tablespoon miso paste
- 1 cup all-purpose flour
- ½ teaspoon coriander seeds
- Sea salt and ground black pepper, to taste
- 1 egg, beaten
- 1 cup bread crumbs
- 2 tablespoons Kewpie Japanese mayonnaise

1. Preheat the air fryer to 400°F (205°C). 2. In a bowl, combine all the ingredients, leaving out the bread crumbs. Press the mixture evenly into a parchment-lined baking pan and freeze until it becomes firm. 3. Once firm, cut the mixture into stick shapes, roll each stick in the bread crumbs, and place them in a lightly greased crisper tray. 4. Insert the crisper tray into the air fryer, select the Air Fry setting, and cook the sticks for about 14 minutes, shaking the tray halfway through for even cooking.

Spiced Potato Bites

Prep time: 5 minutes | Cook time: 14 minutes | Serves 4

- 1 cup mashed boiled potatoes
- 1 cup all-purpose flour
- ½ teaspoon baking powder
- 2 eggs, beaten
- ½ teaspoon cayenne pepper
- ¼ teaspoon dried dill weed
- ½ teaspoon salt
- ¼ teaspoon ground black pepper

1. Preheat the air fryer to 400°F (205°C).2. Combine all ingredients in a bowl, then shape the mixture into bite-sized balls and arrange them in a lightly oiled crisper tray.3. Insert the crisper tray into the air fryer, select the Air Fry function, and cook the sinkers for around 14 minutes, shaking the tray halfway through for even cooking.

Air-Fried Cinnamon Butter Toast

Prep time: 2 minutes | Cook time: 8 minutes | Serves 2

- 2 bread slices
- 1 teaspoon ground cinnamon
- 2 tablespoons butter, softened

1. Preheat the air fryer to 330°F (166°C).2. Coat the bread slices with a mixture of cinnamon and butter, ensuring they are evenly covered, then arrange them in the crisper tray.3. Insert the crisper tray into the air fryer, select the Air Fry function, and cook the bread slices for about 4 minutes; flip them over and continue cooking for another 3 to 4 minutes until golden and crisp.

Feta Green Bean Salad

Prep time: 6 minutes | Cook time: 7 minutes | Serves 4

- 1 pound (454 g) green beans, trimmed
- Sea salt and ground black pepper, to taste
- 1 shallot, finely chopped
- 1 teaspoon minced garlic
- ¼ cup extra-virgin olive oil
- 2 tablespoons white wine vinegar
- ¼ cup chopped fresh parsley
- 2 ounces (57 g) feta cheese, crumbled

1. Start by preheating the air fryer to 375°F (190°C). 2. Arrange the green beans in a lightly greased crisper tray. 3. Place the crisper tray in the corresponding position in the air fryer. Select Air Fry and cook the green beans for 7 minutes; make sure to check the green beans halfway through the cooking time. 4. Add the green beans to a salad bowl; add in the remaining ingredients and stir to combine well. Enjoy!

Herbed Tomato Mozzarella Frittata

Prep time: 5 minutes | Cook time: 15 minutes | Serves 3

- 4 tablespoons sour cream
- 5 eggs
- ¼ cup crumbled Mozzarella cheese
- 2 tablespoons olive oil
- 1 medium tomato, chopped
- ¼ cup chopped fresh parsley
- ¼ cup chopped fresh chives
- ½ teaspoon dried oregano
- Sea salt and ground black pepper, to taste

1. Start by preheating the air fryer to 350ºF (180°C). 2. Spritz the sides and bottom of the baking pan with nonstick cooking oil. 3. In a mixing bowl, thoroughly combine all the ingredients. 4. Pour the mixture into the prepared baking pan. 5. Place the baking pan in the corresponding position in the air fryer. Select Bake and cook the frittata for approximately 15 minutes, or until a toothpick comes out dry and clean.

Cheesy Corn Fritters

Prep time: 5 minutes | Cook time: 15 minutes | Serves 4

- 1 cup all-purpose flour
- ½ teaspoon baking powder
- 1 cup canned sweet corn kernels, drained
- 2 eggs
- ¼ cup buttermilk
- ½ teaspoon sea salt
- ¼ teaspoon freshly ground black pepper, or more to taste
- 1 garlic clove, minced
- 1 tablespoon butter, melted
- 2 ounces (57 g) Swiss cheese, shredded

1. Start by preheating the air fryer to 380ºF (193°C). 2. Mix all the ingredients until everything is well combined. Form the mixture into patties. Transfer to the crisper tray. 3. Place the crisper tray in the corresponding position in the air fryer. Select Air Fry and cook the fritters for about 15 minutes or until cooked through. Turn them over halfway through the cooking time.

Spicy Air-Fried Chickpeas

Prep time: 5 minutes | Cook time: 13 minutes | Serves 4

- 10 ounces (283 g) chickpeas, drained and rinsed
- 1 tablespoon olive oil
- Coarse sea salt and ground
- black pepper, to taste S
- ½ teaspoon garlic powder
- 1 teaspoon cayenne pepper
- ½ teaspoon red chili powder

1. First, preheat the air fryer to 390°F (199°C).2. Toss the chickpeas with the seasonings and spread them evenly in the crisper tray.3. Insert the crisper tray into the air fryer, select the Air Fry setting, and cook for about 13 minutes, shaking the tray a few times to ensure even cooking.

Lemon Garlic Cauliflower Salad

Prep time: 5 minutes | Cook time: 13 minutes | Serves 4

- 1 pound (454 g) cauliflower florets
- Sea salt and ground black pepper, to taste
- 4 tablespoons freshly squeezed lemon juice
- ¼ cup extra-virgin olive oil
- 1 teaspoon minced fresh garlic
- 1 tablespoon chopped fresh parsley
- 2 tablespoons chopped fresh scallions

1. Start by preheating the air fryer to 400°F (205°C). 2. Arrange the cauliflower florets in a lightly greased crisper tray. 3. Place the crisper tray in the corresponding position in the air fryer. Select Air Fry and cook the cauliflower florets for about 13 minutes, shaking the crisper tray halfway through the cooking time. 4. Toss the cauliflower florets with the remaining ingredients.

Ricotta Spinach Frittata

Prep time: 5 minutes | Cook time: 15 minutes | Serves 3

- 6 eggs
- 6 tablespoons half-and-half
- ¼ teaspoon salt
- ¼ teaspoon ground black pepper
- 3 ounces (85 g) ricotta cheese, crumbled
- 2 cups baby spinach
- 1 tablespoon chopped fresh cilantro
- 2 tablespoons olive oil

1. Begin by preheating the air fryer to 350°F (180°C).2. Lightly spray the sides and bottom of the baking pan with nonstick cooking spray to prevent sticking.3. In a mixing bowl, mix all the ingredients together thoroughly until well blended.4. Transfer the mixture into the prepared baking pan.5. Insert the baking pan into the air fryer, select the Bake setting, and cook the frittata for about 15 minutes, or until a toothpick inserted in the center comes out clean and dry.

Zucchini Chickpea Cheese Bites

Prep time: 5 minutes | Cook time: 14 minutes | Serves 4

- 2 eggs, whisked
- ½ cup chickpea flour
- 2 ounces (57 g) feta cheese, crumbled
- 2 ounces (57 g) Swiss cheese, shredded
- 1 bell pepper, chopped
- 1 small zucchini, chopped
- 1 clove garlic, minced
- ½ teaspoon smoked paprika
- Kosher salt and freshly ground black pepper, to taste
- 2 tablespoons butter, melted

1. Start by preheating the air fryer to 400°F (205°C). 2. Mix all the ingredients in a bowl. Shape the mixture into bite-sized balls and place them in a lightly oiled crisper tray. 3. Place the crisper tray in the corresponding position in the air fryer. Select Air Fry and cook the croquettes for about 14 minutes, shaking the crisper tray halfway through the cooking time.

Air-Fried Cinnamon French Toast

Prep time: 5 minutes | Cook time: 8 minutes | Serves 2

- 2 tablespoons butter, melted
- 2 eggs, whisked
- 4 tablespoons coconut milk
- ½ teaspoon ground
- cinnamon
- ½ teaspoon vanilla extract
- 4 tablespoons brown sugar
- 4 slices stale French bread

1. Preheat the air fryer to 330°F (166°C).2. In a mixing bowl, combine the butter, eggs, coconut milk, cinnamon, vanilla extract, and brown sugar until well blended.3. Dip each slice of bread into the egg mixture, ensuring it's fully coated, and then arrange the slices in a lightly greased baking pan.4. Insert the baking pan into the air fryer, select the Bake function, and cook the bread slices for approximately 4 minutes; flip them over and continue cooking for an additional 3 to 4 minutes. Enjoy your delicious treat!

Creamy Basil Egg Salad

Prep time: 5 minutes | Cook time: 15 minutes | Serves 4

- 5 eggs
- 4 tablespoons sour cream
- ¼ cup mayonnaise
- 1 tablespoon Dijon mustard
- 2 tablespoons snipped fresh basil
- Sea salt and ground black pepper, to taste

1. Begin by setting the air fryer to preheat at 270ºF (132ºC). 2. Arrange the eggs carefully onto the crisper tray. 3. Insert the crisper tray into its designated spot within the air fryer. Choose the Air Fry function and allow the eggs to cook for approximately 15 minutes. 4. Once cooked, peel and chop the eggs, then transfer them into a salad bowl. Add the rest of the ingredients and gently mix everything together. 5. Refrigerate the salad until it's time to serve.

Herbed Air-Fried Potato Bites

Prep time: 8 minutes | Cook time: 14 minutes | Serves 4

- ¾ cup all-purpose flour
- 1 cup mashed boiled potatoes
- 2 eggs, whisked
- 1 tablespoon chopped fresh parsley
- 1 tablespoon chopped fresh cilantro
- 2 tablespoons chopped fresh scallions
- Sea salt and ground black pepper, to taste
- ½ cup fresh bread crumbs
- 2 tablespoons olive oil

1. Start by preheating the air fryer to 400ºF (205ºC). 2. Mix all the ingredients in a bowl. Shape the mixture into bite-sized balls and place them in a lightly oiled crisper tray. 3. Place the crisper tray in the corresponding position in the air fryer. Select Air Fry and cook the tater tots for about 14 minutes, shaking the crisper tray halfway through the cooking time.

Sesame Tofu Pepper Bowl

Prep time: 10 minutes | Cook time: 20 minutes | Serves 4

- 2 bell peppers, sliced
- 12 ounces (340 g) firm tofu, pressed and cut into bite-sized cubes
- 2 tablespoons tamari sauce
- 2 tablespoons rice wine
- 2 tablespoons sesame oil
- 1 chili pepper, minced
- 1 garlic clove, minced

1. Start by preheating the air fryer to 390ºF (199ºC). 2. Toss the peppers and tofu with the remaining ingredients in the crisper tray. 3. Place the crisper tray in the corresponding position in the air fryer. Select Air Fry and cook the peppers for about 10 minutes, shaking the crisper tray halfway through the cooking time. 4. Add in the tofu cubes. Reduce the temperature to 360ºF (182ºC). Place the crisper tray in the corresponding position in the air fryer. Select Air Fry and cook for approximately 10 minutes.

Air Fryer Buttermilk Cornbread Bites

Prep time: 5 minutes | Cook time: 15 minutes | Serves 4

- ½ cup corn flour
- ½ cup plain flour
- 1 teaspoon baking soda
- ½ teaspoon salt
- A pinch of grated nutmeg
- 2 eggs, whisked
- 2 tablespoons lard, melted
- 1 cup buttermilk

1. Begin by setting the air fryer to preheat at 350ºF (180ºC). 2. Lightly spray the mini muffin cups with nonstick cooking spray. 3. In a mixing bowl, mix all the ingredients together until well combined. 4. Pour the prepared mixture into the greased mini muffin cups, then place them in the baking pan. 5. Insert the baking pan into the air fryer, select the Bake function, and cook the tartlets for about 15 minutes or until a toothpick inserted into the center comes out clean and dry.

Crispy Broccoli Seed Salad

Prep time: 5 minutes | Cook time: 9 minutes | Serves 4

- 1 pound (454 g) broccoli florets
- 2 tablespoons sunflower seeds
- 2 tablespoons pepitas
- 2 tablespoons Sultanas
- 1 small shallot, chopped
- 1 teaspoon minced garlic
- ¼ cup extra-virgin olive oil
- 1 tablespoon yellow mustard
- Sea salt and ground black pepper, to taste

1. Preheat the air fryer to 395°F (202°C). 2. Arrange the broccoli florets evenly in a greased crisper tray. 3. Insert the crisper tray into the air fryer, set it to Air Fry, and cook the broccoli for 9 minutes, giving the tray a shake halfway through for even crisping. 4. Once cooked, toss the broccoli with the seasonings and other ingredients. Serve at room temperature and enjoy immediately!

Cinnamon Yogurt Pancake Bites

Prep time: 5 minutes | Cook time: 15 minutes | Serves 4

- ¾ cup all-purpose flour
- ½ teaspoon baking powder
- 2 tablespoons brown sugar
- ½ cup yogurt
- 2 eggs, whisked
- ½ teaspoon ground cinnamon
- ½ teaspoon vanilla extract

1. Preheat the air fryer to 360°F (182°C).2. In a bowl, mix all the ingredients until fully combined.3. Spoon the batter onto a greased baking pan, forming small portions.4. Place the baking pan into the air fryer and select the Bake function, cooking for 10 minutes and flipping halfway through.5. Continue with the remaining batter and serve warm. Enjoy!

Air-Fried Sausage Swiss Roll-Ups

Prep time: 5 minutes | Cook time: 10 minutes | Serves 4

- 6 ounces (170 g) refrigerated crescent dinner rolls
- ½ pound (227 g) smoked sausage, chopped
- 4 ounces (113 g) Swiss cheese, shredded
- ½ teaspoon dried oregano
- 2 tablespoons tomato paste

1. Preheat the air fryer to 300°F (150°C).2. Divide the dough into rectangles and mix the remaining ingredients in a bowl.3. Spread the sausage mixture evenly on each rectangle and roll them up tightly.4. Arrange the rolls in a baking pan.5. Insert the pan into the air fryer, select the Bake setting, and cook for 5 minutes, then flip the rolls and bake for another 5 minutes.

Crispy Buckwheat Parmesan Bites

Prep time: 5 minutes | Cook time: 15 minutes | Serves 4

- 1½ cups cooked buckwheat
- 1 cup rice flour
- ½ teaspoon baking powder
- ½ cup grated Parmesan cheese
- 2 eggs, beaten
- 2 tablespoons olive oil
- Sea salt and ground black pepper, to taste

1. Start by preheating the air fryer to 380°F (193°C). 2. Mix all the

ingredients until everything is well combined. Form the mixture into balls. Transfer to the crisper tray. 3. Place the crisper tray in the corresponding position in the air fryer. Select Air Fry and cook the balls for about 15 minutes or until cooked through, shaking the crisper tray halfway through the cooking time.

Feta Spinach Mini Tartlets

Prep time: 5 minutes | Cook time: 15 minutes | Serves 4

- 5 eggs
- 2 tablespoons butter, room temperature
- 1 cup baby spinach
- 1 bell pepper, chopped
- 1 shallot, chopped
- Kosher salt ground black pepper, to taste
- ½ teaspoon dried basil
- ½ teaspoon dried oregano
- 3 ounces (85 g) feta cheese, crumbled

1. Start by preheating the air fryer to 350°F (180°C). 2. Spritz mini muffin cups with nonstick cooking oil. 3. In a mixing bowl, thoroughly combine all the ingredients. 4. Pour the mixture into the prepared mini muffin cups and lower them into the baking pan. 5. Place the baking pan in the corresponding position in the air fryer. Select Bake and cook the tartlets for approximately 15 minutes, or until a toothpick comes out dry and clean.

Mushroom Swiss Frittata Delight

Prep time: 6 minutes | Cook time: 15 minutes | Serves 3

- 6 eggs
- ¼ cup sour cream
- ½ cup shredded Swiss cheese
- Kosher salt and ground black pepper, to taste
- 1 teaspoon hot paprika
- 2 tablespoons olive oil
- 2 cloves garlic, crushed
- 6 ounces (170 g) brown mushrooms, sliced
- 2 tablespoons roughly chopped fresh parsley

1. Preheat the air fryer to 350°F (180°C).2. Lightly spray the sides and bottom of the baking pan with nonstick cooking oil.3. In a bowl, mix all the ingredients until well combined.4. Pour the mixture into the greased baking pan.5. Insert the baking pan into the air fryer, select the Bake function, and cook the frittata for about 15 minutes or until a toothpick inserted comes out clean.

Crispy Air Fryer Panko Arancini

Prep time: 5 minutes | Cook time: 15 minutes | Serves 4

- 1½ cups cooked Arborio rice
- ½ cup grated Parmesan cheese
- 1 cup panko crumbs
- 2 large eggs, whisked
- 1 teaspoon dried parsley flakes
- Kosher salt and freshly ground black pepper, to taste
- 2 tablespoons butter

1. Set the air fryer to preheat at 380°F (193°C). 2. In a bowl, combine all the ingredients thoroughly, then shape the mixture into small balls. Arrange them on the crisper tray. 3. Insert the crisper tray into its proper place in the air fryer. Choose the Air Fry function and cook the balls for around 15 minutes, making sure to shake the tray halfway through to ensure even cooking. Cook until the balls are fully done.

Mushroom Bulgur Fritters

Prep time: 8 minutes | Cook time: 15 minutes | Serves 4

- 1½ cups cooked bulgur
- 1 cup chopped brown mushrooms
- 1 medium onion, chopped
- 2 cloves garlic, finely chopped
- 1 cup crushed crackers
- 2 tablespoons butter
- 2 tablespoons chopped fresh parsley
- Sea salt and ground black pepper, to taste

1. Preheat the air fryer to 380°F (193°C). 2. In a bowl, mix all the ingredients until well combined, then shape the mixture into small balls and arrange them in the crisper tray. 3. Insert the crisper tray into the air fryer, select the Air Fry setting, and cook for about 15 minutes or until fully cooked, shaking the tray midway for even cooking.

Walnut Quinoa Bean Sausages

Prep time: 5 minutes | Cook time: 15 minutes | Serves 4

- 1 cup cooked quinoa
- 10 ounces (283 g) canned red kidney beans, rinsed and dried
- ½ cup ground walnuts
- 1 red onion, chopped
- 2 cloves garlic, minced
- 1 teaspoon smoked paprika
- Sea salt and ground black pepper, to taste

1. Set the air fryer to preheat at 380°F (193°C). 2. Combine all ingredients in a blender or food processor until smooth, then shape the mixture into logs and place them on a greased crisper tray. 3. Insert the crisper tray into the air fryer and choose the Air Fry function. Cook the sausages for roughly 15 minutes, flipping them over halfway to ensure even cooking until they are fully done.

Spinach Egg Cream Cheese Cups

Prep time: 6 minutes | Cook time: 15 minutes | Serves 4

- 4 eggs
- 4 tablespoons cream cheese
- 1 tablespoon butter, melted
- Sea salt and ground black pepper, to taste
- ½ teaspoon cayenne pepper
- 1 cup chopped baby spinach
- 1 small tomato, chopped
- 2 garlic cloves, minced

1. Start by preheating the air fryer to 350ºF (180ºC). 2. Spritz silicone molds with nonstick cooking oil. 3. In a mixing bowl, thoroughly combine all the ingredients. 4. Pour the mixture into the prepared silicone molds and lower them into the baking pan. 5. Place the baking pan in the corresponding position in the air fryer. Select Bake and cook the egg cups for approximately 15 minutes, or until a toothpick comes out dry and clean.

Parmesan Pork and Turkey Meatballs

Prep time: 5 minutes | Cook time: 15 minutes | Serves 4

- ½ pound (227 g) ground pork
- ½ pound (227 g) ground turkey
- 1 onion, minced
- 2 garlic cloves, minced
- ¼ cup Italian-style bread crumbs
- ¼ cup grated Parmesan cheese
- 1 large-sized egg, whisked
- Sea salt and ground black pepper, to taste

1. Start by preheating the air fryer to 380ºF (193ºC). 2. Mix all the ingredients until everything is well combined. Form the mixture into balls. Transfer to the crisper tray. 3. Place the crisper tray in the corresponding position in the air fryer. Select Air Fry and cook the meatballs for about 15 minutes or until cooked through, shaking the crisper tray halfway through the cooking time.

Zesty Zucchini and Gouda Frittata

Prep time: 10 minutes | Cook time: 15 minutes | Serves 4

- 8 eggs
- 6 tablespoons sour cream
- Coarse sea salt and ground black pepper, to taste
- 1 teaspoon cayenne pepper
- ½ teaspoon dried oregano
- 1 teaspoon dried basil
- 4 ounces (113 g) Gouda cheese, shredded
- 2 tablespoons olive oil
- 1 small zucchini, shredded
- 1 small shallot, chopped

1. Begin by preheating the air fryer to 350ºF (180ºC). 2. Lightly coat the bottom and sides of the baking pan with nonstick cooking spray. 3. In a bowl, mix all the ingredients together until fully blended. 4. Pour the combined mixture into the greased baking pan. 5. Place the baking pan into its proper position inside the air fryer, select the Bake function, and cook the frittata for about 15 minutes, or until a toothpick inserted into the center comes out clean and dry.

Chapter 2

Beans and Grains

Chapter 2 Beans and Grains

Cinnamon Fig Bread Pudding

Prep time: 10 minutes | Cook time: 20 minutes | Serves 5

8 slices bread, cubed	chopped
1 cup milk	A pinch of sea salt
2 eggs, beaten	½ teaspoon ground cinnamon
¼ cup brown sugar	
2 ounces (57 g) dried figs,	½ teaspoon vanilla extract

1. Arrange the bread cubes in a lightly greased baking pan.2. In a mixing bowl, thoroughly mix the remaining ingredients until well combined.3. Pour the milk mixture over the bread cubes, ensuring they are evenly soaked. Allow to sit for 15 minutes to absorb the liquid.4. Preheat the air fryer to 350°F (180°C).5. Insert the baking pan into the air fryer, select the Bake setting, and cook the bread pudding for about 20 minutes or until the custard is set but still slightly wobbly in the center.6. Serve warm or at room temperature. Enjoy!

Vanilla Cinnamon Cornbread Casserole

Prep time: 5 minutes | Cook time: 12 minutes | Serves 6

3 eggs	½ teaspoon ground cinnamon
2 tablespoons coconut oil, room temperature	A pinch of grated nutmeg
½ cup heavy cream	A pinch of salt
1 teaspoon vanilla	6 slices sweet cornbread
½ cup brown sugar	

1. Begin by preheating the air fryer to 330°F (166°C).2. In a mixing bowl, whisk together the eggs, coconut oil, heavy cream, vanilla extract, sugar, cinnamon, nutmeg, and salt until well combined.3. Arrange the cornbread slices in a lightly greased baking pan and pour the custard mixture evenly over them.4. Insert the baking pan into the air fryer, select the Bake function, and cook the casserole for approximately 12 minutes. Enjoy your delicious dish!

Mozzarella Mac and Cheese Bake

Prep time: 5 minutes | Cook time: 15 minutes | Serves 4

2 cups macaroni	seasoning
1 cup milk	Sea salt and ground black pepper, to taste
2 cups grated Mozzarella cheese	½ teaspoon garlic powder
½ teaspoon Italian	1 teaspoon dry mustard

1. Start by preheating the air fryer to 360°F (182°C). 2. Cook the macaroni according to the package directions. 3. Drain the macaroni and place them in a lightly greased baking pan. 4. Fold in the remaining ingredients and stir to combine. 5. Place the baking pan in the corresponding position in the air fryer. Select Bake and cook the mac and cheese for about 15 minutes. Serve garnished with fresh Italian herbs, if desired.

Crispy Cabbage Butter Fritters

Prep time: 10 minutes | Cook time: 15 minutes | Serves 4

1 cup rice flour	½ cup shredded green cabbage
4 tablespoons chickpea flour	1 teaspoon onion powder
½ teaspoon sweet paprika	1 teaspoon garlic powder
1 teaspoon chili powder	2 tablespoons butter
Sea salt and ground black pepper, to taste	½ cup vegetable broth

1. Preheat the air fryer to 380°F (193°C). 2. In a bowl, thoroughly mix all the ingredients and shape the mixture into patties. Place the patties on the crisper tray. 3. Insert the crisper tray into the air fryer, select the Air Fry setting, and cook the patties for approximately 15 minutes, flipping them halfway through to ensure even cooking until they're fully done.

Creamy Corn Butter Fritters

Prep time: 5 minutes | Cook time: 15 minutes | Serves 4

- 1 cup canned and creamed corn kernels
- 1 cup whole-wheat flour
- 1 teaspoon baking powder
- 2 eggs, whisked
- ½ cup heavy cream
- 2 tablespoons butter

1. Start by preheating the air fryer to 380°F (193°C). 2. Mix all ingredients until everything is well combined. Form the mixture into patties. Transfer to the crisper tray. 3. Place the crisper tray in the corresponding position in the air fryer. Select Air Fry and cook the fritters for about 15 minutes or until cooked through. Turn them over halfway through the cooking time.

Mediterranean Sour Cream Biscuits

Prep time: 5 minutes | Cook time: 15 minutes | Serves 6

- 1 cup all-purpose flour
- 1 teaspoon baking powder
- 4 tablespoons olive oil
- ½ cup sour cream
- A pinch of sea salt
- 1 teaspoon Mediterranean seasoning mix

1. Start by preheating the air fryer to 360°F (182°C). 2. Mix all ingredients until well combined. Use a 2-inch biscuit cutter and cut out biscuits. Place the biscuits in a lightly greased baking pan. 3. Place the baking pan in the corresponding position in the air fryer. Select Bake and cook the biscuits for about 15 minutes or until a tester comes out dry and clean.

Pumpkin Spice Cranberry Granola

Prep time: 10 minutes | Cook time: 15 minutes | Serves 6

- ½ cup rolled oats
- ¼ cup toasted wheat germ
- ½ cup dried cranberries
- ¼ cup pumpkin seeds
- ¼ cup sunflower seeds
- ¼ cup chopped pecans
- ¼ cup chopped walnuts
- ½ teaspoon vanilla extract
- ¼ cup agave syrup
- 4 tablespoons coconut oil
- 1 teaspoon pumpkin pie spice mix

1. Start by preheating the air fryer to 350°F (180°C). 2. Thoroughly combine all ingredients in a lightly greased baking pan. 3. Place the baking pan in the corresponding position in the air fryer. Select Bake and cook the granola for about 15 minutes, stirring every 5 minutes. 4. Store at room temperature in an airtight container for up to three weeks.

Honey Coconut Prune Bread Pudding

Prep time: 10 minutes | Cook time: 20 minutes | Serves 5

- 8 slices bread, cubed
- 1 cup coconut milk
- ¼ cup coconut oil
- 1 egg, beaten
- ¼ cup honey
- ½ teaspoon ground cinnamon
- ¼ teaspoon ground cloves
- A pinch of kosher salt
- ½ cup pitted and chopped prunes

1. Arrange the bread cubes in a lightly greased baking pan. 2. In a mixing bowl, whisk together the milk, coconut oil, egg, honey, cinnamon, cloves, and salt until well combined. 3. Pour the custard mixture over the bread cubes and gently fold in the prunes. Allow the mixture to sit for 15 minutes to soak. 4. Preheat the air fryer to 350°F (180°C). 5. Insert the baking pan into the air fryer, select the Bake setting, and cook the bread pudding for approximately 20 minutes or until the custard is set but still slightly wobbly in the center. Enjoy!

Honey Vanilla Doughnut Pudding

Prep time: 8 minutes | Cook time: 20 minutes | Serves 6

- 2 cups diced doughnuts
- 2 eggs, whisked
- 1 cup milk
- 1 cup half-and-half
- 4 tablespoons honey
- 1 teaspoon vanilla extract
- A pinch of salt
- A pinch of grated nutmeg

1. Arrange the doughnuts in a lightly greased baking pan. 2. In a mixing bowl, mix together the remaining ingredients until thoroughly combined. 3. Pour the custard mixture over the doughnuts and let them soak for 15 minutes. 4. Preheat the air fryer to 350°F (180°C). 5. Insert the baking pan into the air fryer, select the Bake setting, and cook for about 20 minutes or until the custard is set but still slightly wobbly in the center. 6. Serve warm or at room temperature. Enjoy!

Buttermilk Raisin Scones

Prep time: 15 minutes | Cook time: 17 minutes | Serves 6

1 cup all-purpose flour	2 egg, beaten
1 teaspoon baking powder	¼ cup buttermilk
¼ teaspoon salt	½ teaspoon vanilla extract
¼ teaspoon grated nutmeg	6 tablespoons raisins, soaked for 15 minutes
½ cup brown sugar	

1. Begin by preheating the air fryer to 360°F (182°C).2. In a mixing bowl, combine all the ingredients until fully incorporated. Spoon the batter into baking cups and place them into the baking pan.3. Insert the baking pan into the air fryer, select the Bake setting, and cook the scones for approximately 17 minutes, or until a toothpick inserted comes out clean. Enjoy your freshly baked scones!

Mocha Cocoa Muffins

Prep time: 5 minutes | Cook time: 15 minutes | Serves 6

½ cup coconut flour	A pinch of grated nutmeg
½ cup all-purpose flour	1 tablespoon instant coffee granules
½ cup cocoa powder	½ cup milk
½ cup brown sugar	2 eggs, whisked
½ teaspoon baking powder	½ teaspoon vanilla extract
A pinch of sea salt	

1. Preheat the air fryer to 330°F (166°C).2. Combine all the ingredients in a mixing bowl until well blended, then divide the batter evenly into silicone baking molds and place them in a baking pan.3. Insert the baking pan into the air fryer, select the Bake setting, and cook the muffins for approximately 15 minutes, or until a toothpick inserted comes out clean.4. Let the muffins cool slightly before removing them from the molds and serving. Enjoy!

Cinnamon Vanilla Air-Fried Toast

Prep time: 5 minutes | Cook time: 8 minutes | Serves 3

2 eggs	¼ teaspoon grated nutmeg
½ cup milk	½ teaspoon cinnamon powder
2 tablespoons butter, room temperature	3 slices challah bread
1 teaspoon vanilla extract	

1. Start by preheating the air fryer to 330°F (166°C). 2. In a mixing bowl, thoroughly combine the eggs, milk, butter, vanilla, nutmeg, and cinnamon. 3. Then dip each piece of bread into the egg mixture; place the bread slices in a lightly greased crisper tray. 4. Place the crisper tray in the corresponding position in the air fryer. Select Air Fry and cook the bread slices for about 4 minutes; turn them over and cook for a further 3 to 4 minutes. Enjoy!

Tropical Pineapple Coconut Oatmeal

Prep time: 5 minutes | Cook time: 12 minutes | Serves 4

1 cup old-fashioned oats	1 cup coconut milk
1 teaspoon baking powder	1 cup pineapple juice
½ teaspoon cinnamon	¼ cup agave syrup
A pinch of sea salt	2 tablespoons ground chia seeds
A pinch of grated nutmeg	1 teaspoon vanilla extract

1. Preheat the air fryer to 380°F (193°C).2. In a mixing bowl, thoroughly combine all the ingredients until well blended. Spoon the mixture into lightly greased mugs.3. Arrange the mugs in a baking pan.4. Insert the baking pan into the air fryer, select the Bake setting, and cook the oatmeal for approximately 12 minutes. Enjoy your delicious oatmeal!

Lemon Blueberry Cream Cheese Rolls

Prep time: 5 minutes | Cook time: 10 minutes | Serves 6

1 (8-ounce / 227-g) can refrigerated crescent dinner rolls	1 teaspoon grated lemon zest
6 ounces (170 g) cream cheese, room temperature	1 cup fresh blueberries
4 tablespoons granulated sugar	1 cup powdered sugar
	¼ teaspoon ground cinnamon

1. Start by preheating the air fryer to 300°F (150°C). 2. Separate the dough into rectangles. Mix the remaining ingredients until well combined. 3. Spread each rectangle with the cheese mixture; roll them up tightly. 4. Place the rolls in the baking pan. 5. Place the baking pan in the corresponding position in the air fryer. Select Bake and cook the rolls for about 5 minutes; turn them over and bake for a further 5 minutes.

Spicy Curry Basmati Rice

Prep time: 10 minutes | Cook time: 10 minutes | Serves 4

3 tablespoons olive oil	chopped
3 cloves garlic, chopped	2 cups basmati rice, cooked
1 large onion, peeled and chopped	1 teaspoon cayenne pepper
1 sprigs fresh curry leaves,	Kosher salt and ground black pepper, to taste

1. Begin by preheating the air fryer to 360ºF (182ºC). 2. In a lightly greased baking pan, mix all the ingredients together, then pour 1 cup of boiling water over the rice. 3. Insert the baking pan into its proper place in the air fryer, select the Bake function, and cook for approximately 10 minutes or until the rice is fully cooked.

Herbed Scallion Rice Pilaf

Prep time: 10 minutes | Cook time: 10 minutes | Serves 4

1½ cups cooked multigrain rice	1 tablespoon chopped fresh cilantro
1 cup vegetable broth	2 tablespoons olive oil
½ cup thinly sliced scallions	Sea salt and cayenne pepper, to taste
1 tablespoon chopped fresh parsley	1 teaspoon garlic powder

1. Start by preheating the air fryer to 360ºF (182ºC). 2. Thoroughly combine all ingredients in a lightly greased baking pan. 3. Place the baking pan in the corresponding position in the air fryer. Select Bake and cook for about 10 minutes or until cooked through.

Honey Chocolate Chip Muffins

Prep time: 5 minutes | Cook time: 15 minutes | Serves 6

½ cup all-purpose flour	¼ cup honey
⅓ cup almond flour	¼ cup milk
1 teaspoon baking powder	1 teaspoon vanilla extract
A pinch of sea salt	4 tablespoons coconut oil
A pinch of grated nutmeg	½ cup dark chocolate chips
1 egg	

1. Preheat the air fryer to 320ºF (160ºC). 2. In a bowl, combine all the ingredients thoroughly. Spoon the batter into silicone baking molds and set them inside the baking pan. 3. Place the baking pan into the air fryer, select the Bake setting, and cook the muffins for around 15 minutes, or until a tester inserted in the center comes out clean and dry. 4. Let the muffins cool down before removing them from the molds and serving.

Cinnamon Apple Cream Cheese Rolls

Prep time: 5 minutes | Cook time: 10 minutes | Serves 5

1 (8-ounce / 227-g) can crescent rolls	cheese, room temperature
	¼ cup sugar
1 teaspoon ground cinnamon	2 tablespoons full-fat milk
4 ounces (113 g) cream	½ cup canned apple pie filling

1. Preheat the air fryer to 300ºF (150ºC). 2. Divide the dough into rectangles and mix the remaining ingredients thoroughly until combined. 3. Spread the cinnamon mixture evenly over each rectangle, then roll them up tightly. 4. Arrange the rolls in the baking pan. 5. Insert the baking pan into the air fryer, select the Bake function, and cook the rolls for 5 minutes. Flip them over and bake for an additional 5 minutes until fully cooked.

Honey Almond Baked Oatmeal

Prep time: 5 minutes | Cook time: 12 minutes | Serves 4

1 cup rolled oats	A pinch of kosher salt
1 cup water	½ teaspoon ground cloves
1 cup milk	4 tablespoons honey
1 teaspoon vanilla paste	½ cup slivered almonds

1. Begin by preheating the air fryer to 380°F (193°C). 2. In a mixing bowl, mix all the ingredients together until well combined. Spoon the mixture into lightly greased ramekins. 3. Arrange the ramekins in a baking pan. 4. Insert the baking pan into the air fryer, select the Bake setting, and cook the oatmeal for approximately 12 minutes. Serve warm or at room temperature. Enjoy!

Spiced Paneer Rice Fritters

Prep time: 5 minutes | Cook time: 15 minutes | Serves 4

1 cup rice flour	2 tablespoons butter, room temperature
½ onion, chopped	1 teaspoon paprika
2 garlic cloves, minced	1 teaspoon cumin powder

½ cup crumbled Paneer cheese

1. Preheat the air fryer to 380°F (193°C). 2. Combine all the ingredients in a bowl, mixing thoroughly, then shape the mixture into patties. Arrange the patties on the crisper tray. 3. Insert the crisper tray into the air fryer and select the Air Fry function. Cook the patties for about 15 minutes, flipping them halfway through to ensure even cooking, until they are fully cooked.

Creamy Pancetta Carbonara Risotto

Prep time: 10 minutes | Cook time: 10 minutes | Serves 4

2 cups Arborio rice, cooked	taste
2 tablespoons sesame oil	4 tablespoons chopped pancetta
1 shallot, chopped	1 cup grated Parmesan cheese
½ cup white Italian wine	1 tablespoon chopped fresh Italian parsley
½ cup heavy cream	
Coarse sea salt and freshly ground black pepper, to	

1. Preheat the air fryer to 360°F (182°C). 2. In a lightly greased baking pan, mix all the ingredients together until well combined. 3. Place the baking pan in its proper position inside the air fryer, select the Bake setting, and cook for approximately 10 minutes, or until the dish is fully cooked.

Spicy Cheesy Butter Macaroni

Prep time: 5 minutes | Cook time: 15 minutes | Serves 4

1 cups macaroni	cheese, crumbled
1 cup cream of onion soup	Kosher salt and ground white pepper, to taste
2 tablespoons butter	½ teaspoon ground cumin
4 ounces (113 g) Ricotta cheese	1 teaspoon dry mustard
6 ounces (170 g) Mozzarella	1 teaspoon red chili powder

1. Preheat the air fryer to 360°F (182°C). 2. Cook the macaroni as per the package instructions. 3. After draining, transfer the macaroni to a lightly greased baking pan. 4. Add the remaining ingredients and stir everything together until well combined. 5. Place the baking pan into the air fryer, select the Bake function, and cook the mac and cheese for around 15 minutes. Serve with a garnish of fresh Italian herbs, if desired.

Golden Corn Koftas

Prep time: 10 minutes | Cook time: 15 minutes | Serves 5

6 ounces (170 g) canned corn kernels	mint
½ small-sized onion, peeled and chopped	2 tablespoons butter, melted
2 cloves garlic, minced	2 eggs, beaten
2 tablespoons chopped fresh parsley	½ cup rice flour
2 tablespoons chopped fresh	1 teaspoon baking powder
	Sea salt and ground black pepper, to taste
	1 teaspoon turmeric powder

1. Preheat the air fryer to 380°F (193°C). 2. In a bowl, combine all the ingredients and mix thoroughly, then shape the mixture into balls. Arrange the balls on the crisper tray. 3. Place the crisper tray into the air fryer, select the Air Fry function, and cook for about 15 minutes, tossing the tray halfway through to ensure even cooking until the balls are fully cooked.

Cinnamon Apple Oat Muffins

Prep time: 8 minutes | Cook time: 15 minutes | Serves 6

½ cups self-rising flour	½ cup milk
½ cup rolled oats	¼ cup coconut oil, room temperature
½ cup agave syrup	2 eggs
¼ teaspoon grated nutmeg	1 teaspoon coconut extract
½ teaspoon cinnamon powder	1 cup cored and chopped apples
A pinch of coarse salt	

1. Start by preheating the air fryer to 320°F (160°C). 2. Mix all ingredients in a bowl. 3. Scrape the batter into silicone baking molds; place them in the baking pan. 4. Place the baking pan in the corresponding position in the air fryer. Select Bake and cook the muffins for about 15 minutes or until a tester comes out dry and clean. 5. Allow the muffins to cool before unmolding and serving.

Chapter

3

Poultry

Chapter 3 Poultry

Garlic Butter Chicken Breasts

Prep time: 5 minutes | Cook time: 12 minutes | Serves 4

- 1 pound (454 g) chicken breasts, boneless and skinless
- 1 tablespoon butter, room temperature
- 1 teaspoon garlic powder
- Kosher salt and ground black pepper, to taste
- 1 teaspoon dried parsley flakes
- 1 teaspoon smoked paprika
- ½ teaspoon dried oregano

1. Begin by preheating the air fryer to 380°F (193°C).2. Use kitchen towels to pat the chicken breasts dry, then toss them with the remaining ingredients until evenly coated. Arrange the chicken breasts in the crisper tray.3. Insert the crisper tray into the air fryer, select the Air Fry setting, and cook the chicken for 12 minutes, flipping them over halfway through the cooking time for even browning. Enjoy your meal!

Marinated Rice Wine Chicken Breasts

Prep time: 5 minutes | Cook time: 12 minutes | Serves 4

- 1 pound (454 g) chicken breasts, boneless, skinless
- ½ cup rice wine
- 1 tablespoon stone-ground mustard
- 1 teaspoon minced garlic
- 1 teaspoon whole black peppercorns
- 1 teaspoon chili powder
- ¼ teaspoon sea salt, or more to taste

1. Place the chicken, wine, mustard, garlic, and whole peppercorns in a ceramic bowl. Cover the bowl and let the chicken marinate for about 3 hours in the refrigerator. 2. Preheat the air fryer to 380°F (193°C). 3. Discard the marinade and place the chicken breasts in the crisper tray. 4. Place the crisper tray in the corresponding position in the air fryer. Select Roast and cook the chicken breasts for 12 minutes, turning them over halfway through the cooking time. 5. Season the chicken with the chili powder and salt. Serve immediately and enjoy!

Crispy Turkey Schnitzel

Prep time: 5 minutes | Cook time: 22 minutes | Serves 3

- 1½ pounds (680 g) turkey thighs, skinless, boneless
- 1 egg, beaten
- ½ cup all-purpose flour
- ½ cup seasoned bread crumbs
- ½ teaspoon crushed red pepper flakes
- Sea salt and ground black pepper, to taste
- 1 tablespoon olive oil

1. Start by preheating the air fryer to 380°F (193°C). 2. Flatten the turkey thighs with a mallet. 3. Whisk the egg in a shallow bowl. Place the flour in a second bowl. 4. Then, in a third shallow bowl, place the bread crumbs, red pepper, salt, and black pepper. Dip the turkey first in the flour, then, in the beaten egg, and roll them in the bread crumb mixture. 5. Place the breaded turkey thighs in the crisper tray and mist them with the olive oil. 6. Place the crisper tray in the corresponding position in the air fryer. Select Air Fry and cook the schnitzel for 22 minutes, turning them over halfway through the cooking time.

Spicy Chicken Cheddar Sliders

Prep time: 5 minutes | Cook time: 17 minutes | Serves 4

- 1 pound (454 g) ground chicken
- ½ cup crushed tortilla chips
- 2 ounces (57 g) Cheddar cheese, grated
- 1 teaspoon dried parsley
- flakes
- 1 teaspoon cayenne pepper
- ½ teaspoon paprika
- Kosher salt and ground black pepper, to taste
- 4 dinner rolls

1. Preheat the air fryer to 380°F (193°C). 2. In a bowl, combine the chicken, crushed tortilla chips, cheese, and spices, mixing thoroughly. Shape the mixture into four even patties. 3. Place the patties on the crisper tray, spacing them out. 4. Insert the crisper tray into the air fryer, select the Air Fry setting, and cook the burgers for about 17 minutes, flipping them halfway through to ensure even cooking. 5. Once cooked, serve the burgers on dinner rolls.

Cheesy Italian Chicken Fillets

Prep time: 5 minutes | Cook time: 12 minutes | Serves 4

- 1½ pounds (680 g) chicken fillets
- 2 tablespoons olive oil
- 1 teaspoon smoked paprika
- 1 teaspoon Italian seasoning
- mix
- Sea salt and ground black pepper, to taste
- ½ cup grated Pecorino Romano cheese

1. Start by preheating the air fryer to 380°F (193°C). 2. Pat the chicken fillets dry with paper towels. Toss the chicken fillets with the olive oil and spices. Place the chicken fillets in the crisper tray. 3. Place the crisper tray in the corresponding position in the air fryer. Select Air Fry and cook the chicken fillets for 12 minutes, turning them over halfway through the cooking time. 4. Top the chicken fillets with grated cheese and serve warm.

Herbed Breaded Chicken Schnitzel

Prep time: 5 minutes | Cook time: 20 minutes | Serves 3

- 3 chicken legs, boneless and skinless
- 2 tablespoons olive oil
- 1 teaspoon dried basil
- 1 teaspoon dried oregano
- 1 teaspoon dried sage
- Sea salt and freshly cracked black pepper
- ½ cup bread crumbs

1. Preheat the air fryer to 370°F (188°C). 2. Use paper towels to pat the chicken legs dry, then toss them with the remaining ingredients until well coated. 3. Arrange the chicken legs in the crisper tray. 4. Insert the crisper tray into the air fryer, select the Air Fry function, and cook the chicken for 20 minutes, flipping them over halfway through to ensure even cooking. Enjoy!

Parmesan Garlic Chicken Wings

Prep time: 5 minutes | Cook time: 22 minutes | Serves 3

- 1 pound (454 g) chicken wings, bone-in
- Sea salt and red pepper flakes, to taste
- 2 tablespoons olive oil
- ½ cup grated Parmesan cheese
- 2 cloves garlic, pressed

1. Start by preheating the air fryer to 380°F (193°C). 2. Pat the chicken wings dry with kitchen towels. Toss the chicken wings with the remaining ingredients. 3. Arrange the chicken wings in the crisper tray. 4. Place the crisper tray in the corresponding position in the air fryer. Select Air Fry and cook the chicken wings for 22 minutes, turning them over halfway through the cooking time.

Honey Soy Duck Fillet

Prep time: 5 minutes | Cook time: 30 minutes | Serves 4

- 1½ pounds (680 g) duck fillet
- 1 tablespoon honey
- 2 tablespoons dark soy sauce
- 1 tablespoon soybean paste

1. Preheat the air fryer to 330°F (166°C). 2. Toss the duck fillet with the remaining ingredients until evenly coated, then place the fillet in the baking pan. 3. Insert the baking pan into the air fryer, select the Bake setting, and cook the duck fillet for 15 minutes, turning it over halfway through the cooking time. 4. After 15 minutes, increase the temperature to 350°F (180°C) and continue cooking for about 15 minutes or until the duck is fully cooked. 5. Allow the duck to rest for 10 minutes before carving and serving. Enjoy your meal!

Sun-Dried Tomato and Mozzarella Stuffed Chicken

Prep time: 10 minutes | Cook time: 20 minutes | Serves 4

- 1 pound (454 g) chicken breasts, boneless, skinless, cut into 4 pieces
- 2 tablespoons chopped sun-dried tomatoes
- 1 garlic clove, minced
- 2 ounces (57 g) Mozzarella cheese, crumbled
- Sea salt and ground black pepper, to taste
- 1 tablespoon olive oil

1. First, set your air fryer to preheat at 400°F (205°C) to create the perfect cooking environment. 2. Take a mallet and gently pound the chicken breasts to flatten them evenly. 3. Carefully fill each chicken breast with sun-dried tomatoes, minced garlic, and your choice of cheese. Roll the chicken tightly and secure the rolls with toothpicks to keep the filling inside. 4. Generously season the outside of the chicken rolls with salt and pepper, then drizzle olive oil on top for added flavor. 5. Arrange the stuffed chicken in the crisper tray, ensuring they are positioned securely. Insert the crisper tray into the air fryer and choose the Air Fry setting. Cook the chicken for approximately 20 minutes, flipping them halfway through for even cooking. Savor the delicious flavors of your stuffed chicken!

Greek-Seasoned Chicken Fillets

Prep time: 5 minutes | Cook time: 12 minutes | Serves 4

1½ pounds (680 g) chicken fillets	seasoning mix
1 tablespoon olive oil	½ teaspoon crushed red pepper flakes
1 teaspoon minced garlic	Sea salt and ground black pepper, to taste
1 tablespoon Greek	

1. Start by preheating the air fryer to 380°F (193°C). 2. Pat the chicken dry with paper towels. Toss the chicken with the remaining ingredients. 3. Arrange the chicken in the crisper tray. 4. Place the crisper tray in the corresponding position in the air fryer. Select Roast and cook the chicken fillets for 12 minutes, turning them over halfway through the cooking time.

Rotisserie Lemon Oregano Chicken

Prep time: 10 minutes | Cook time: 1½ hours | Serves 4

1 whole chicken (3 to 3½ pounds / 1.4 to 1.6 kg)

Rub:

⅓ cup finely chopped fresh oregano	1 tablespoon olive oil
2 cloves garlic, minced	2 teaspoons kosher salt
Zest of 1 lemon	¼ teaspoon freshly ground black pepper

Baste:

Juice of 1 lemon	vinegar
1 tablespoon chopped fresh oregano	1 teaspoon sugar
	¼ teaspoon salt
1 tablespoon white wine	1 lemon (for cavity)

1. Prepare the Rub: In a small bowl, mix the rub ingredients together to create a wet paste. Pat the chicken dry with paper towels and generously apply the rub all over, including under the breast skin. Place the chicken on a large plate, cover it with plastic wrap, and refrigerate for 4 hours. 2. Make the Baste: In another small bowl, combine all the baste ingredients and set aside. 3. Bring to Room Temperature: Take the chicken out of the refrigerator and let it sit at room temperature for 20 minutes. 4. Preheat the Air Fryer: Set the air fryer to 400°F (205°C) to preheat. 5. Truss the Chicken: Use kitchen twine to truss the chicken. Run the rotisserie spit through a lemon and insert it into the chicken cavity, using a paring knife to create a pilot hole in the lemon for easier insertion. Continue to run the spit through the chicken and secure it with

the rotisserie forks. 6. Cook the Chicken: Place the chicken on the preheated grill, positioning a drip tray underneath. Add 1 cup of hot water to the tray. Select the Rotisserie function and cook the chicken for 1½ hours. Baste the chicken during the last 30 minutes of cooking until the meat in the thighs and legs reaches 175°F (79°C), and the breasts reach 165°F (74°C). 7. Rest and Carve: Once done, carefully remove the chicken from the heat, take out the rotisserie forks, and slide the spit out. Place the chicken on a large cutting board, tent it with aluminum foil, and let it rest for 15 to 20 minutes before cutting off the twine and carving. Enjoy your delicious rotisserie chicken!

Spicy Hot Chicken Thighs

Prep time: 5 minutes | Cook time: 22 minutes | Serves 4

1 pound (454 g) chicken thighs, bone-in	2 tablespoons olive oil
Sea salt and freshly ground black pepper, to taste	1 teaspoon stone-ground mustard
	¼ cup hot sauce

1. Preheat the air fryer to 380°F (193°C). 2. Use kitchen towels to pat the chicken dry, then toss it with the remaining ingredients until well coated. Arrange the chicken in the crisper tray. 3. Insert the crisper tray into the air fryer, select the Air Fry setting, and cook the chicken for 22 minutes, flipping it over halfway through the cooking time for even cooking. Enjoy your meal!

Avocado Turkey Sliders

Prep time: 8 minutes | Cook time: 20 minutes | Serves 4

1 pound (454 g) ground turkey	2 garlic cloves, minced
1 tablespoon olive oil	½ cup bread crumbs
1 avocado, peeled, pitted, and chopped	Kosher salt and ground black pepper, to taste
	8 small rolls

1. Start by preheating the air fryer to 380°F (193°C). 2. Mix the turkey, olive oil, avocado, garlic, bread crumbs, salt, and black pepper until everything is well combined. Form the mixture into eight small patties. 3. Arrange the patties in the crisper tray. 4. Place the crisper tray in the corresponding position in the air fryer. Select Air Fry and cook the patties for about 20 minutes or until cooked through; make sure to turn them over halfway through the cooking time. 5. Serve the patties in the prepared rolls and enjoy!

Spicy Cayenne Chicken Legs

Prep time: 5 minutes | Cook time: 30 minutes | Serves 4

4 chicken legs, bone-in	½ teaspoon mustard seeds
2 tablespoons sesame oil	1 teaspoon cayenne pepper
Coarse sea salt and ground black pepper, to taste	½ teaspoon onion powder
	½ teaspoon garlic powder

1. Start by preheating the air fryer to 380ºF (193ºC). 2. Pat the chicken dry with paper towels. Toss the chicken legs with the remaining ingredients. Arrange the chicken legs in the crisper tray. 3. Place the crisper tray in the corresponding position in the air fryer. Select Air Fry and cook the chicken for 30 minutes, turning them over halfway through the cooking time.

Lemon Cream Chicken Salad

Prep time: 5 minutes | Cook time: 12 minutes | Serves 4

1 pound (454 g) chicken breasts, skinless and boneless	1 tablespoon lemon juice
¼ cup mayonnaise	Sea salt and ground black pepper, to taste
¼ cup sour cream	½ cup chopped celery

1. Start by preheating the air fryer to 380ºF (193ºC). 2. Pat the chicken dry with paper towels. Place the chicken in a lightly oiled crisper tray. 3. Place the crisper tray in the corresponding position in the air fryer. Select Roast and cook the chicken breasts for 12 minutes, turning them over halfway through the cooking time. 4. Shred the chicken breasts using two forks; transfer it to a salad bowl and add in the remaining ingredients. 5. Toss to combine and serve chilled.

Five-Spice Sesame Chicken Drumsticks

Prep time: 5 minutes | Cook time: 22 minutes | Serves 3

3 chicken drumsticks	1 tablespoon soy sauce
2 tablespoons sesame oil	1 teaspoon five-spice powder
Kosher salt and ground black pepper, to taste	

1. Begin by setting your air fryer to preheat at 370ºF (188ºC) to ensure it's ready for cooking. 2. Next, thoroughly dry the chicken drumsticks using paper towels. In a large bowl, combine the chicken drumsticks with the remaining ingredients, ensuring they are well-coated. Arrange the seasoned drumsticks in the crisper tray, making sure they're evenly spaced. 3. Insert the crisper tray into the designated position within the air fryer. Select the Roast function and let the chicken cook for 22 minutes, flipping them halfway through the cooking process to achieve an even crispiness. Enjoy your perfectly roasted chicken drumsticks!

Smoky Butter Chicken Cutlets

Prep time: 8 minutes | Cook time: 12 minutes | Serves 4

1 pound (454 g) chicken breasts, boneless, skinless, cut into 4 pieces	1 teaspoon smoked paprika
1 tablespoon butter, melted	Kosher salt and ground black pepper, to taste
	1 teaspoon garlic powder

1. Start by preheating the air fryer to 380ºF (193ºC). 2. Flatten the chicken breasts to ¼-inch thickness. 3. Toss the chicken breasts with the remaining ingredients. 4. Arrange the chicken breasts in the crisper tray. 5. Place the crisper tray in the corresponding position in the air fryer. Select Roast and cook the chicken for 12 minutes, turning them over halfway through the cooking time.

Cheddar Chicken Muffin Melts

Prep time: 5 minutes | Cook time: 12 minutes | Serves 4

1 pound (454 g) chicken breasts	4 slices Cheddar cheese
1 tablespoon olive oil	4 teaspoons yellow mustard
Sea salt and black pepper, to taste	4 English muffins, lightly toasted

1. To begin, preheat your air fryer to 380ºF (193ºC) so it's hot and ready for the chicken. 2. Use kitchen towels to pat the chicken dry, ensuring it's moisture-free. In a mixing bowl, combine the chicken breasts with olive oil, salt, and pepper, tossing until they are evenly coated. Transfer the seasoned chicken into the crisper tray. 3. Insert the crisper tray into its designated position in the air fryer. Select the Roast setting and cook the chicken for 12 minutes, flipping the pieces halfway through for a balanced cook. 4. Once cooked, use two forks to shred the chicken into bite-sized pieces. Serve it alongside cheese, mustard, and toasted English muffins for a delightful meal!

Roasted Chicken and Carrot Salad

Prep time: 10 minutes | Cook time: 12 minutes | Serves 3

¾ 1 pound (454 g) chicken breast	½ cup mayonnaise
2 tablespoons chopped scallions	1 tablespoon mustard
1 carrot, shredded	Sea salt and ground black pepper, to taste

1. Start by preheating the air fryer to 380ºF (193ºC). 2. Pat the chicken dry with kitchen towels. Place the chicken in a lightly oiled crisper tray. 3. Place the crisper tray in the corresponding position in the air fryer. Select Roast and cook the chicken for 12 minutes, turning them over halfway through the cooking time. 4. Chop the chicken breasts and transfer it to a salad bowl; add in the remaining ingredients and toss to combine well.

Peruvian Rotisserie Chicken

Prep time: 5 minutes | Cook time: 1½ hours | Serves 4

1 whole chicken (3½ to 4 pounds / 1.6 to 1.8 kg)	

Marinade:

¼ cup white vinegar	1 tablespoon sweet paprika
¼ cup dry white wine	1 tablespoon ground cumin
2 tablespoons olive oil	1 teaspoon freshly ground black pepper
3 or 4 cloves garlic, minced	1¼ teaspoons salt

1. Prepare the marinade by mixing all the marinade ingredients in a bowl and set aside. 2. Trim any excess skin from the chicken and pat it dry with paper towels, both inside and out. Place the chicken in a large resealable bag or a nonreactive bowl. Pour the marinade over the chicken, and use tongs to turn and coat the chicken thoroughly. Seal the bag or cover the bowl with plastic wrap, then refrigerate for 6 to 8 hours. 3. Preheat the air fryer to 400ºF (205ºC). 4. Truss the chicken with kitchen twine and run the rotisserie spit through the chicken, securing it with the forks. If any marinade remains, brush it onto the chicken. 5. Place the chicken in the preheated air fryer and set a drip tray underneath. Select the Rotisserie setting and cook for 70 to 90 minutes, or until the thigh reaches an internal temperature of at least 175ºF (79ºC), while the breast reaches 165ºF (74ºC). 6. Once cooked, carefully remove the chicken from the heat, take out the rotisserie forks, and slide out the spit. Place the chicken on a cutting board, tent it with aluminum foil, and let it rest for 10 minutes before removing the twine and carving.

Red Wine Marinated Turkey Wings

Prep time: 5 minutes | Cook time: 40 minutes | Serves 5

2 pounds (907 g) turkey wings, bone-in	½ cup red wine
2 garlic cloves, minced	Sea salt and ground black pepper, to taste
1 small onion, chopped	1 teaspoon poultry seasoning
1 tablespoon Dijon mustard	

1. In a ceramic bowl, combine the turkey wings, garlic, onion, mustard, and wine. Cover the bowl and allow the turkey to marinate in the refrigerator overnight.2. Preheat the air fryer to 400°F (205°C).3. After marinating, discard the marinade and season the turkey wings with salt, black pepper, and poultry seasoning, tossing to coat evenly.4. Arrange the seasoned turkey wings in the crisper tray.5. Insert the crisper tray into the air fryer, select the Air Fry function, and cook the turkey wings for 40 minutes, turning them over halfway through for even cooking. Enjoy your delicious turkey wings!

Air-Fried Chicken Pepper Fajitas

Prep time: 10 minutes | Cook time: 30 minutes | Serves 4

1 pound (454 g) chicken legs, boneless, skinless, cut into pieces	1 jalapeño pepper, sliced
	1 onion, sliced
2 tablespoons canola oil	½ teaspoon onion powder
1 red bell pepper, sliced	½ teaspoon garlic powder
1 yellow bell pepper, sliced	Sea salt and ground black pepper, to taste

1. Preheat the air fryer to 380°F (193°C).2. Use paper towels to pat the chicken legs dry, then toss them with 1 tablespoon of canola oil. Arrange the chicken in the crisper tray.3. Insert the crisper tray into the air fryer, select the Air Fry function, and cook the chicken for 15 minutes, shaking the tray halfway through for even cooking.4. After 15 minutes, add the remaining ingredients to the crisper tray, increase the temperature to 400°F (205°C), and continue air frying for another 15 minutes or until the chicken is fully cooked. Enjoy!

Balsamic Glazed Chicken Drumettes

Prep time: 5 minutes | Cook time: 22 minutes | Serves 4

1½ pounds (680 g) chicken drumettes	2 tablespoons balsamic vinegar
2 tablespoons olive oil	Kosher salt and ground black pepper, to taste

1. Preheat the air fryer to 380°F (193°C). 2. In a bowl, toss the chicken drumettes with all the remaining ingredients until well coated. 3. Arrange the seasoned chicken drumettes in the crisper tray, spacing them evenly. 4. Insert the crisper tray into the air fryer, select the Roast setting, and cook the drumettes for 22 minutes, flipping them halfway through to ensure even cooking.

Herb-Buttered Turkey Breasts

Prep time: 5 minutes | Cook time: 1 hour | Serves 5

2 pounds (907 g) turkey breasts, rib bones trimmed	1 tablespoon chopped fresh parsley
4 tablespoons butter, melted	1 tablespoon chopped fresh thyme
1 teaspoon Sriracha sauce	Kosher salt and freshly ground black pepper, to taste
1 tablespoon chopped fresh cilantro	

1. Preheat the air fryer to 350°F (180°C). 2. Use paper towels to pat the turkey breasts dry. In a bowl, toss the turkey breasts with the remaining ingredients until evenly coated. Arrange the turkey breasts in the crisper tray. 3. Insert the crisper tray into the air fryer, select the Roast function, and cook the turkey breasts for 1 hour, flipping them every 20 minutes for even cooking.

Spicy Mustard Chicken Breasts

Prep time: 5 minutes | Cook time: 12 minutes | Serves 2

¾ pound (340 g) chicken breasts, boneless, skinless	¼ cup hot sauce
1 teaspoon minced garlic	1 tablespoon Dijon mustard
½ cup red wine	Sea salt and cayenne pepper, to taste

1. In a ceramic bowl, combine the chicken, garlic, red wine, hot sauce, and mustard. Cover the bowl and allow the chicken to marinate in the refrigerator for about 3 hours. 2. Preheat the air fryer to 380°F (193°C). 3. After marinating, discard the marinade and place the chicken breasts in the crisper tray. 4. Insert the crisper tray into the air fryer, select the Roast setting, and cook the chicken breasts for 12 minutes, flipping them halfway through for even cooking. 5. Once cooked, season the chicken with salt and cayenne pepper to taste.

Hawaiian Glazed Rotisserie Chicken

Prep time: 10 minutes | Cook time: 1 to 1½ hours | Serves 4

Sauce:

Juice of 4 large limes	2 cloves garlic, minced
½ cup soy sauce	1½ teaspoons sesame oil
¼ cup honey	¼ teaspoon freshly ground black pepper
3 tablespoons ketchup	¼ teaspoon red pepper flakes
3 tablespoons packed dark brown sugar	

Chicken:

1 whole chicken (3 to 3½ pounds / 1.4 to 1.6 kg)	¼ teaspoon freshly ground black pepper
¼ teaspoon salt	1 large onion, peeled but left whole (for cavity)

1. Prepare the sauce by mixing the sauce ingredients in a medium bowl. Split the mixture into two equal parts; set aside one half for basting and use the other half as a marinade. 2. Place the chicken in a large resealable plastic bag or a nonreactive bowl, then pour the marinade over the chicken. Use tongs to ensure the chicken is well coated. Seal the bag or cover the bowl, and refrigerate for 1 to 2 hours. 3. Preheat the air fryer to 400°F (205°C). 4. After marinating, remove the chicken from the bag, discarding the marinade. Pat the chicken dry inside and out with paper towels, then season with salt and pepper. Truss the chicken using kitchen twine. Insert the rotisserie spit through the onion and into the cavity of the chicken; a paring knife can help create a pilot hole in the onion for easier insertion. Continue inserting the spit through the chicken and secure it with the rotisserie forks. 5. Place the chicken on the preheated grill, setting a drip tray underneath. Select the Rotisserie function and cook for 1 to 1½ hours, or until the thighs and legs reach an internal temperature of 175°F (79°C) and the breasts reach 165°F (74°C). Begin basting the chicken with the reserved sauce during the last 30 minutes of cooking. 6. Once cooked, remove the chicken from the heat, carefully take out the rotisserie forks, and slide the spit out. Place the chicken on a large cutting board, tent it with aluminum foil, and let it rest for 15 to 20 minutes before removing the twine and carving.

Crispy Buttermilk Chicken Breasts

Prep time: 5 minutes | Cook time: 12 minutes | Serves 4

- 1 pound (454 g) chicken breast halves
- Sea salt and ground black pepper, to taste
- 1 cup buttermilk
- 1 cup all-purpose flour
- ½ teaspoon onion powder
- 1 teaspoon garlic powder

1 teaspoon smoked paprika

1. In a large bowl, combine the chicken pieces with salt and black pepper, tossing to coat evenly. Pour in the buttermilk and mix until the chicken is coated on all sides. Cover and refrigerate for about 6 hours. 2. Preheat the air fryer to 380ºF (193ºC). 3. In a shallow bowl, mix together the flour, onion powder, garlic powder, and smoked paprika until well combined. 4. Dredge the marinated chicken in the seasoned flour, shaking off any excess, then place the pieces on a lightly oiled crisper tray. 5. Insert the crisper tray into the air fryer, select the Air Fry setting, and cook the chicken for 12 minutes, flipping them halfway through for even cooking. 6. Serve and enjoy!

Herb-Roasted Turkey Drumsticks

Prep time: 5 minutes | Cook time: 40 minutes | Serves 5

- 2 pounds (907 g) turkey drumsticks, bone-in
- 2 tablespoons olive oil
- Kosher salt and freshly ground black pepper, to
- taste
- 1 teaspoon dried thyme
- 1 teaspoon dried rosemary
- 1 teaspoon minced garlic

1. Preheat the air fryer to 400ºF (205ºC). 2. In a bowl, toss the turkey drumsticks with all the remaining ingredients until well coated. Arrange the drumsticks on the crisper tray. 3. Insert the crisper tray into the air fryer, select the Air Fry setting, and cook the turkey drumsticks for 40 minutes, flipping them over halfway through to ensure even cooking.

Greek Chicken Cucumber Salad

Prep time: 10 minutes | Cook time: 12 minutes | Serves 4

- 1 pound (454 g) chicken breasts, boneless, skinless
- 1 red onion, thinly sliced
- 1 bell pepper, sliced
- 4 Kalamata olives, pitted and minced
- 1 small Greek cucumber,
- grated and squeezed
- 4 tablespoons Greek yogurt
- 4 tablespoons mayonnaise
- 1 tablespoon fresh lemon juice
- Coarse sea salt and red pepper flakes, to taste

1. Preheat the air fryer to 380ºF (193ºC). 2. Use paper towels to pat the chicken breasts dry, then arrange them in a lightly oiled crisper tray. 3. Insert the crisper tray into the air fryer, select the Roast setting, and cook the chicken for 12 minutes, flipping them halfway through to ensure even cooking. 4. Once cooked, chop the chicken breasts and transfer them to a salad bowl. Add the remaining ingredients and toss everything together until well combined. 5. Serve the salad chilled.

Spicy Pineapple Chicken Legs

Prep time: 5 minutes | Cook time: 35 minutes | Serves 4

- 1 pound (454 g) chicken legs, boneless
- Kosher salt and freshly ground black pepper, to taste
- 2 tablespoons tamari sauce
- 1 tablespoon hot sauce
- 1 cup peeled and diced pineapple
- 1 tablespoon roughly chopped fresh cilantro

1. Preheat the air fryer to 380ºF (193ºC). 2. Pat the chicken legs dry using paper towels. In a bowl, toss the chicken with salt, black pepper, tamari sauce, and hot sauce until evenly coated. Arrange the chicken legs on the crisper tray. 3. Insert the crisper tray into the air fryer, select the Roast function, and cook the chicken for 30 minutes, flipping them over halfway through the cooking time. 4. After 30 minutes, top the chicken with pineapple and continue cooking for an additional 5 minutes. Serve warm, garnished with fresh cilantro.

Chapter 4

Beef, Pork, and Lamb

Chapter 4 Beef, Pork, and Lamb

Spicy Beef Burger Buns

Prep time: 5 minutes | Cook time: 15 minutes | Serves 3

¾ pound (340 g) ground beef	Sea salt and ground black pepper, to taste
2 tablespoons minced onion	1 teaspoon red chili powder
1 teaspoon minced garlic	3 hamburger buns
1 teaspoon cayenne pepper	

1. First, preheat your air fryer to 380ºF (193ºC) to get it ready for cooking. 2. In a mixing bowl, combine the ground beef, finely chopped onion, minced garlic, cayenne pepper, salt, black pepper, and red chili powder. Mix thoroughly until all ingredients are well integrated. Shape the mixture into three equal patties and arrange them in the crisper tray. 3. Insert the crisper tray into the designated slot in the air fryer. Set the Air Fry function and cook the burgers for about 15 minutes, ensuring to flip them halfway through to guarantee even cooking. 4. Once done, serve the juicy burgers on your prepared buns and savor every bite!

Espresso-Rubbed Sirloin Roast

Prep time: 10 minutes | Cook time: 1 hour | Serves 6

1 sirloin roast (3 pounds / 1.4 kg)
Rub:

2 tablespoons ground espresso	1 tablespoon kosher salt
3 or 4 cloves garlic, minced	2 teaspoons onion powder
1½ tablespoons balsamic vinegar	2 teaspoons freshly ground black pepper
1 tablespoon olive oil	1 teaspoon Worcestershire sauce

1. Begin by preheating your air fryer to a sizzling 400ºF (205ºC) to prepare for the roast. 2. Use paper towels to thoroughly pat the roast dry. To create a pilot hole, insert a long sword skewer through the center of the roast lengthwise. Then, slide the rotisserie spit through this hole and secure it with the provided forks, making sure it's balanced properly. 3. Prepare the rub by combining all the rub ingredients in a bowl and generously applying it all over the surface of the meat. To ensure a consistent shape during cooking, tie the roast with twine. 4. Place the seasoned roast on the preheated grill, setting a drip tray underneath. Pour 1 to 2 cups of hot water into the tray, replenishing it as needed. Select the Rotisserie setting and cook the roast for 60 to 70 minutes, or until it reaches your preferred doneness: 125ºF (52ºC) for rare, 135ºF (57ºC) for medium rare, 145ºF (63ºC) for medium, 155ºF (68ºC) for medium well, or 165ºF (74ºC) for well done. Remember, the roast will shrink as it cooks, so adjust the forks accordingly. 5. Once cooked, carefully detach the rotisserie forks and slide the spit out. Place the roast on a large cutting board and tent it with aluminum foil, allowing it to rest for 15 to 20 minutes. Remove the twine and slice the roast for serving. For sandwiches, aim to slice the meat as thinly as possible to enhance flavor in every bite!

Blue Cheese Pork Tenderloin with Mushrooms

Prep time: 10 minutes | Cook time: 15 minutes | Serves 4

1½ pounds (680 g) pork tenderloin	2 tablespoons olive oil
Sea salt and ground black pepper, to taste	1 pound (454 g) mushrooms, sliced
	2 ounces (57 g) blue cheese

1. Begin by preheating your air fryer to an impressive 400ºF (205ºC) to get it ready for the pork. 2. In a mixing bowl, season the pork with salt, black pepper, and olive oil, ensuring it is well-coated. Carefully transfer the seasoned pork to a crisper tray that has been lightly greased. 3. Insert the crisper tray into the appropriate slot in the air fryer. Set the Air Fry function and cook the pork for 10 minutes, remembering to turn them over halfway through to ensure even cooking. 4. After 10 minutes, layer the pork with fresh mushrooms and continue cooking for an additional 5 minutes. Once finished, sprinkle warm blue cheese over the top for a rich and savory finish. Enjoy your deliciously cooked pork!

Garlic-Infused Pork Ribs

Prep time: 5 minutes | Cook time: 35 minutes | Serves 4

● 1½ pounds (680 g) St. Louis-style ribs	● Kosher salt and ground black pepper, to taste
● 1 teaspoon hot sauce	● 2 garlic cloves, minced
● 1 tablespoon canola oil	

1. Start by preheating the air fryer to 350ºF (180ºC). 2. Toss all ingredients in a lightly greased crisper tray. 3. Place the crisper tray in the corresponding position in the air fryer. Select Roast and cook the pork ribs for 35 minutes, turning them over halfway through the cooking time.

Citrus-Marinated Cuban Pork Tenderloin

Prep time: 10 minutes | Cook time: 1 hour | Serves 6

● 2 large pork tenderloins (about 3½ pounds / 1.6 kg each)	

Marinade:

● ½ cup freshly squeezed orange juice	flakes
● ¼ cup freshly squeezed lime juice	● 1¼ teaspoons salt
● 1 tablespoon vegetable oil	● ½ teaspoon freshly ground black pepper
● 3 cloves garlic, grated	● 2 tablespoons chopped fresh cilantro, for garnish
● ½ teaspoon ground cumin	● 2 limes, quartered, for serving
● ½ teaspoon red pepper	

1. Cut off any excess fat and remove the silverskin from the tenderloins. Place in a large resealable plastic bag or glass baking dish. 2. Make the marinade: Combine the marinade ingredients in a bowl and pour over the pork. Using tongs, gently turn the pork to coat. Seal the bag or cover the dish with plastic wrap. Place in the refrigerator for 4 to 8 hours. Remove from the refrigerator 30 minutes before you're ready to cook. Drain the tenderloins and pat dry with paper towels. 3. Preheat the air fryer to 400ºF (205ºC). 4. Place the tenderloins on a large cutting board, large end to small end, making one uniform roast. Season with the salt and pepper. Tie together with kitchen twine every 2 inches. Run a long sword skewer through the center of the roasts lengthwise to create a pilot hole. Run the rotisserie spit through the hole and secure with the forks. Balance as necessary. 5. Place the tenderloins on the air fryer with a drip tray underneath. Select Rotisserie and cook for 45 to 60 minutes, or until the internal temperature at the thickest part reaches 140ºF to 145ºF (60ºC to 63ºC). The roast will shrink during cooking, so adjust the forks when appropriate. 6. Remove from the heat, carefully remove the rotisserie forks and slide the spit out, and then set the tenderloins on a large cutting board. Tent the roast with aluminum foil and let the meat rest for 15 to 20 minutes. 7. Cut away the twine and carve the tenderloins into thin slices. Garnish with the cilantro and serve with the lime wedges.

Beef and Broccoli Patties

Prep time: 10 minutes | Cook time: 15 minutes | Serves 4

● 1 pound (454 g) beef	● 2 garlic cloves, minced
● ½ pound (227 g) broccoli, minced	● Sea salt and ground black pepper, to taste
● 1 small onion, chopped	● 1 tablespoon tamari sauce

1. Start by preheating the air fryer to 380ºF (193ºC). 2. In a mixing bowl, thoroughly combine all ingredients . Shape the mixture into four patties. Arrange the patties in the crisper tray. 3. Place the crisper tray in the corresponding position in the air fryer. Select Air Fry and cook the burgers for about 15 minutes or until cooked through; make sure to turn them over halfway through the cooking time. 4. Serve the warm patties with the topping of choice.

Lime-Glazed Ham with Spices

Prep time: 5 minutes | Cook time: 1 hour | Serves 4

● 1½ pounds (680 g) ham	mustard
● ¼ cup sherry wine	● A pinch of grated nutmeg
● 2 tablespoons dark brown sugar	● ½ teaspoon ground cloves
● 2 tablespoons freshly squeezed lime juice	● ¼ teaspoon ground cardamom
● 1 tablespoon stone-ground	● ½ teaspoon ground black pepper, or more to taste

1. Start by preheating the air fryer to 400ºF (205ºC). 2. In a mixing bowl, whisk all the remaining ingredients to make the glaze. 3. Wrap the ham in a piece of aluminum foil and lower it into the crisper tray. Reduce the temperature to 375ºF (190ºC). Place the crisper tray in the corresponding position in the air fryer. Select Air Fry and cook the ham for about 30 minutes. 4. Remove the foil, increase the temperature to 400ºF (205ºC), and continue to cook an additional 15 minutes, coating the ham with the glaze every 5 minutes.

Sesame Garlic Beef Tenderloin

Prep time: 10 minutes | Cook time: 20 minutes | Serves 4

♦ 1½ pounds (680 g) beef tenderloin, sliced	♦ 2 garlic cloves, minced
♦ 2 tablespoons sesame oil	♦ 1 teaspoon peeled and grated fresh ginger
♦ 1 teaspoon five-spice powder	♦ 2 tablespoons soy sauce

1. First, preheat your air fryer to a hot 400°F (205°C) to prepare for cooking. 2. In a mixing bowl, combine the beef tenderloin with the remaining ingredients, tossing well to ensure it's thoroughly coated. Carefully place the seasoned beef tenderloin into the crisper tray. 3. Insert the crisper tray into its designated position in the air fryer. Select the Air Fry setting and cook the beef tenderloin for 20 minutes, flipping it halfway through to achieve even cooking. 4. Once done, serve and enjoy the juicy, flavorful beef tenderloin!

Smoked Sausage with Crispy Onion Rings

Prep time: 5 minutes | Cook time: 15 minutes | Serves 4

♦ 1 pound (454 g) pork sausage, smoked	♦ 4 ounces (113 g) onion rings

1. Start by preheating the air fryer to 370°F (188°C). 2. Place the sausage in a lightly greased crisper tray. 3. Place the crisper tray in the corresponding position in the air fryer. Select Air Fry and cook the sausage for approximately 7 minutes, tossing crisper tray halfway through the cooking time. 4. Add in the onion rings and continue to cook for 8 minutes more.

T-bone Steak Salad with Tomato and Lime

Prep time: 10 minutes | Cook time: 12 minutes | Serves 5

♦ 2 pounds (907 g) T-bone steak	♦ ¼ cup extra-virgin olive oil
♦ 1 teaspoon garlic powder	♦ 1 bell pepper, seeded and sliced
♦ Sea salt and ground black pepper, to taste	♦ 1 red onion, sliced
♦ 2 tablespoons lime juice	♦ 1 tomato, diced

1. Begin by preheating your air fryer to a sizzling 400°F (205°C) to create the perfect cooking atmosphere. 2. In a bowl, season the steak with garlic powder, salt, and black pepper, tossing well to ensure an even coating. Place the seasoned steak in the crisper tray for cooking. 3. Insert the crisper tray into the appropriate slot in the air fryer. Select the Air Fry setting and cook the steak for 12 minutes, making sure to turn it over halfway through for optimal browning. 4. After cooking, slice the steak into pieces and mix in the remaining ingredients. Serve it at room temperature or well chilled for a refreshing dish!

Garlic-Spiced Skirt Steak

Prep time: 5 minutes | Cook time: 12 minutes | Serves 4

♦ 1½ pounds (680 g) skirt steak	♦ 1 teaspoon cayenne pepper
♦ Kosher salt and freshly cracked black pepper, to taste	♦ ¼ teaspoon cumin powder
	♦ 2 tablespoons olive oil
	♦ 2 garlic cloves, minced

1. Start by preheating the air fryer to 400°F (205°C). 2. Toss the steak with the other ingredients; place the steak in the crisper tray. 3. Place the crisper tray in the corresponding position in the air fryer. Select Air Fry and cook the steak for 12 minutes, turning it over halfway through the cooking time.

Herbed Pork Chops with Bell Peppers

Prep time: 8 minutes | Cook time: 15 minutes | Serves 4

♦ 1½ pounds (680 g) center-cut rib chops	♦ Kosher salt and freshly ground black pepper, to taste
♦ 2 bell peppers, seeded and sliced	♦ 1 teaspoon chopped fresh rosemary
♦ 2 tablespoons olive oil	♦ 1 teaspoon chopped fresh basil
♦ ½ teaspoon mustard powder	

1. Begin by setting your air fryer to preheat at 400°F (205°C) to prepare for cooking. 2. In a lightly greased crisper tray, combine all the ingredients and toss them together until they are evenly mixed. 3. Insert the crisper tray into the appropriate position in the air fryer. Choose the Air Fry setting and cook the pork chops along with the bell peppers for 15 minutes, making sure to flip them halfway through the cooking time for optimal browning. Enjoy your flavorful pork chops and bell peppers!

Smoky Paprika Pork Loin Chops

Prep time: 5 minutes | Cook time: 15 minutes | Serves 4

- 1 pound (454 g) pork loin chops
- 1 tablespoon olive oil
- Sea salt and ground black pepper, to taste
- 1 tablespoon smoked paprika

1. First, preheat your air fryer to a blazing 400ºF (205ºC) to set the stage for cooking. 2. In a lightly greased crisper tray, combine all the ingredients, ensuring they are evenly distributed for the best flavor. 3. Insert the crisper tray into its designated position in the air fryer. Select the Air Fry setting and cook the pork loin chops for 15 minutes, remembering to flip them halfway through to achieve an even cook. Enjoy your deliciously prepared pork loin chops!

Butter-Basted Coulotte Roast

Prep time: 5 minutes | Cook time: 55 minutes | Serves 5

- 2 pounds (907 g) Coulotte roast
- 2 tablespoons butter
- Kosher salt and ground
- black pepper, to taste
- 1 teaspoon ground allspice
- 1 teaspoon minced garlic

1. Start by preheating the air fryer to 390ºF (199ºC). 2. Toss the beef with the remaining ingredients; place the beef in the crisper tray. 3. Place the crisper tray in the corresponding position in the air fryer. Select Roast and cook the beef for 55 minutes, turning it over halfway through the cooking time. 4. Enjoy!

Spicy Bacon and Tomato Sandwich

Prep time: 8 minutes | Cook time: 10 minutes | Serves 3

- 6 ounces (170 g) thick-cut bacon
- 2 tablespoons brown sugar
- 2 teaspoons chipotle chile powder
- 1 teaspoon cayenne pepper
- 1 tablespoon Dijon mustard
- 1 heads lettuce, torn into leaves
- 2 medium tomatoes, sliced
- 6 (½-inch) slices white bread

1. Begin by preheating your air fryer to a high temperature of 400ºF (205ºC) to prepare for cooking. 2. In a bowl, combine the bacon with sugar, chipotle chile powder, cayenne pepper, and mustard, tossing until the bacon is well coated with the mixture. 3. Arrange the seasoned bacon in the crisper tray and place the tray into its designated position in the air fryer. Select the Air Fry function and cook the bacon for about 10 minutes, making sure to toss the crisper tray halfway through for even cooking. 4. Once cooked, assemble your sandwiches by layering the crispy bacon with fresh lettuce and ripe tomato for a delicious meal!

Herb-Roasted Rosemary Pork Belly

Prep time: 5 minutes | Cook time: 45 minutes | Serves 5

- 1 pound (454 g) pork belly
- 1 tablespoon tomato sauce
- 2 tablespoons rice vinegar
- 1 teaspoon dried thyme
- 1 teaspoon dried rosemary

1. First, preheat your air fryer to 320ºF (160ºC) to create the perfect cooking environment. 2. In a lightly greased baking pan, combine all the ingredients and toss them together until evenly mixed. 3. Insert the baking pan into the appropriate position in the air fryer. Select the Bake setting and cook the pork belly for 20 minutes. After that, carefully turn it over and continue cooking for an additional 25 minutes to achieve a crispy texture. 4. Once cooked, serve the pork belly warm and savor every delicious bite!

Herb-Crusted Pork Burgers

Prep time: 15 minutes | Cook time: 15 minutes | Serves 4

- 1 pound (454 g) ground pork
- 1 small onion, chopped
- 1 garlic clove, minced
- 4 tablespoons crushed tortilla chips
- 1 teaspoon minced fresh sage
- 1 teaspoon minced fresh coriander
- 1 tablespoon minced fresh parsley
- 1 egg, beaten
- ½ teaspoon smoked paprika
- Sea salt and freshly ground black pepper, to taste

1. Start by preheating the air fryer to 380ºF (193ºC). 2. In a mixing bowl, thoroughly combine all ingredients . Form the mixture into four patties. Arrange the patties in the crisper tray. 3. Place the crisper tray in the corresponding position in the air fryer. Select Air Fry and cook the burgers for about 15 minutes or until cooked through; make sure to turn them over halfway through the cooking time.

Garlic Rosemary Pork Shoulder Chops

Prep time: 5 minutes | Cook time: 15 minutes | Serves 4

1½ pounds (680 g) pork shoulder chops	black pepper, to taste
2 tablespoons olive oil	2 sprigs rosemary, leaves picked and chopped
Kosher salt and ground	1 teaspoon crushed garlic

1. Preheat the air fryer to 400°F (205°C). 2. In a lightly greased crisper tray, toss together all the ingredients until well combined. 3. Insert the crisper tray into the air fryer and select the Air Fry setting. Cook the pork shoulder chops for 15 minutes, flipping them halfway through the cooking time for even browning.

Balsamic-Glazed Rotisserie Beef Roast

Prep time: 10 minutes | Cook time: 50 minutes | Serves 6

1 chuck roast (3 to 3½ pounds / 1.4 to 1.6 kg)	
Glaze:	
¾ cup balsamic vinegar	½ teaspoon Worcestershire sauce
3 tablespoons packed brown sugar	
Rub:	
2 teaspoons kosher salt	1 teaspoon freshly ground black pepper
1½ teaspoons onion powder	½ teaspoon garlic powder

1. To prepare the glaze, combine all the glaze ingredients in a saucepan over medium heat. Simmer for 5 to 6 minutes, stirring frequently to prevent burning; adjust the heat as necessary. The mixture should remain runny, resembling a mop sauce rather than a thick glaze. Once done, cover the pot and remove it from the heat, allowing it to cool. 2. Trim any excess fat from the surface of the roast and place it on a large cutting board. Using kitchen twine, start from the center and tie the roast into a round shape, ensuring it's tight. You will need about five ties to achieve the proper roundness. To create a pilot hole, insert a long skewer lengthwise through the center of the roast, then slide the rotisserie spit through the hole and secure it with the forks, adjusting for balance as needed. 3. Preheat the air fryer to 400°F (205°C). 4. For the rub, mix all the rub ingredients in a small bowl and apply the mixture generously over the roast. 5. Place the roast in the preheated air fryer, setting a drip tray underneath. Select the Rotisserie setting and cook for 50 to 70 minutes, depending on your desired doneness: 125°F (52°C) for rare, 135°F (57°C) for medium rare, 145°F (63°C) for medium,

155°F (68°C) for medium well, or 165°F (74°C) for well done. After the first 25 minutes, begin basting the roast generously with the glaze every 10 minutes until it's fully cooked. 6. Once done, remove the roast from the heat, carefully take out the rotisserie forks, and slide out the spit. Place the roast on a large cutting board, tent it with aluminum foil, and let it rest for 10 to 15 minutes. After resting, cut off the twine and slice the meat into ⅓- to ½-inch thick pieces before serving.

Garlic-Infused Picnic Ham

Prep time: 5 minutes | Cook time: 1 hour | Serves 4

1½ pounds (680 g) picnic ham	2 garlic cloves, minced
	2 tablespoons rice vinegar
2 tablespoons olive oil	1 tablespoon tamari sauce

1. Preheat the air fryer to 400°F (205°C). 2. In a bowl, toss the ham with the remaining ingredients, then wrap it tightly in a piece of aluminum foil and place it in the crisper tray. 3. Lower the temperature to 375°F (190°C) and insert the crisper tray into the air fryer. Select the Air Fry setting and cook the ham for approximately 30 minutes. 4. After 30 minutes, carefully remove the foil, increase the temperature back to 400°F (205°C), and continue cooking for an additional 15 minutes, or until the ham is fully cooked through.

Herb-Crusted Oregano Beef Brisket

Prep time: 10 minutes | Cook time: 1 hour | Serves 4

1½ pounds (680 g) beef brisket	½ teaspoon ground cumin
2 tablespoons olive oil	2 cloves garlic, minced
Sea salt and freshly ground black pepper, to taste	2 tablespoons chopped chives
1 teaspoon dried oregano	2 tablespoons chopped cilantro
1 teaspoon mustard powder	

1. Preheat the air fryer to 390°F (199°C). 2. In a bowl, toss the beef brisket with the remaining ingredients until well coated, then place the brisket in the crisper tray. 3. Insert the crisper tray into the air fryer, select the Roast setting, and cook the beef brisket for 15 minutes. After 15 minutes, flip the beef over and reduce the temperature to 360°F (182°C). 4. Continue cooking the brisket for about 55 minutes, or until it is fully cooked through. 5. Once done, shred the beef using two forks and serve with your choice of toppings.

Garlic Rosemary Ribeye Steak

Prep time: 5 minutes | Cook time: 15 minutes | Serves 4

1 pound (454 g) ribeye steak, bone-in	Sea salt and ground black pepper, to taste
2 tablespoons butter, room temperature	2 rosemary sprigs, leaves picked and chopped
2 garlic cloves, minced	

1. Preheat the air fryer to 400°F (205°C). 2. In a bowl, toss the ribeye steak with butter, garlic, salt, black pepper, and rosemary until well coated. Place the seasoned steak in the crisper tray. 3. Insert the crisper tray into the air fryer, select the Air Fry setting, and cook the ribeye steak for 15 minutes, flipping it halfway through for even cooking.

Thyme-Infused Beef Brisket

Prep time: 5 minutes | Cook time: 1 hour | Serves 4

1½ pounds (680 g) beef brisket	Sea salt and ground black pepper, to taste
2 tablespoons olive oil	1 teaspoon dried parsley flakes
1 teaspoon onion powder	
1 teaspoon garlic powder	1 teaspoon dried thyme

1. Preheat the air fryer to 390°F (199°C). 2. In a bowl, toss the beef with all the remaining ingredients until well coated, then transfer the beef to the crisper tray. 3. Insert the crisper tray into the air fryer, select the Roast setting, and cook the beef for 15 minutes. After 15 minutes, flip the beef over and lower the temperature to 360°F (182°C). 4. Continue cooking the beef for an additional 55 minutes, or until it reaches the desired tenderness.

Maple Bacon Roasted Cauliflower

Prep time: 10 minutes | Cook time: 12 minutes | Serves 4

1 pound (454 g) bacon, cut into thick slices	1 teaspoon paprika
1 pound (454 g) cauliflower, cut into florets	Kosher salt and ground black pepper, to taste
1 tablespoon maple syrup	2 cloves garlic, minced

1. Preheat the air fryer to 400°F (205°C). 2. In the crisper tray, toss together all the ingredients until well combined. 3. Insert the crisper tray into the air fryer, select the Air Fry setting, and cook the bacon and cauliflower for about 12 minutes, flipping them halfway through for even cooking. 4. Serve immediately.

Sage-Infused Pork with Applesauce Glaze

Prep time: 5 minutes | Cook time: 55 minutes | Serves 5

1 tablespoon olive oil	taste
2 tablespoons soy sauce	2 cloves garlic, smashed
2 pounds (907 g) pork butt	2 sprigs fresh sage, chopped
Kosher salt and freshly ground black pepper, to	1 cup applesauce

1. Preheat the air fryer to 360°F (182°C). 2. In a lightly greased crisper tray, toss together all the ingredients except for the applesauce. 3. Insert the crisper tray into the air fryer, select the Air Fry setting, and cook the pork butt for 45 minutes, flipping it halfway through for even cooking. 4. After 45 minutes, top the pork butt with the applesauce and continue cooking for an additional 10 minutes. 5. Allow the pork to rest for a few minutes before slicing and serving.

Spicy Pork and Beef Burgers

Prep time: 8 minutes | Cook time: 15 minutes | Serves 5

1 pound (454 g) ground pork	5 tablespoons crushed tortilla chips
½ pound (227 g) ground beef	2 tablespoons olive oil
½ cup chopped scallions	Sea salt and ground black pepper, to taste
1 teaspoon minced garlic	5 ciabatta rolls
1 tablespoon Sriracha sauce	

1. Preheat the air fryer to 380°F (193°C). 2. In a mixing bowl, combine the meat, scallions, garlic, Sriracha sauce, crushed tortilla chips, olive oil, salt, and black pepper until well mixed. Shape the mixture into four patties. 3. Place the patties in the crisper tray, ensuring they are spaced apart. 4. Insert the crisper tray into the air fryer, select the Air Fry setting, and cook the burgers for about 15 minutes, flipping them halfway through for even cooking. 5. Serve the burgers on ciabatta rolls.

Dijon Mustard-Crusted Pork Loin

Prep time: 5 minutes | Cook time: 55 minutes | Serves 4

- 1½ pounds (680 g) pork top loin
- 1 tablespoon olive oil
- 1 tablespoon Dijon mustard
- 2 cloves garlic, crushed
- 1 tablespoon parsley
- 1 tablespoon coriander
- ½ teaspoon crushed red pepper flakes
- Kosher salt and ground black pepper, to taste

1. Preheat the air fryer to 360°F (182°C). 2. In a lightly greased crisper tray, toss all the ingredients together until evenly coated. 3. Insert the crisper tray into the air fryer, select the Air Fry setting, and cook the pork for 55 minutes, flipping it halfway through for even cooking. 4. Serve warm and enjoy your dish!

Habanero-Spiced Beef Meatloaf

Prep time: 10 minutes | Cook time: 25 minutes | Serves 4

- 1½ pounds (680 g) ground chuck
- ½ onion, chopped
- 1 teaspoon minced habanero pepper
- ¼ cup crushed tortilla chips
- 1 teaspoon minced garlic
- Sea salt and ground black pepper, to taste
- 2 tablespoons olive oil
- 1 egg, whisked

1. Preheat the air fryer to 390°F (199°C). 2. In a mixing bowl, combine all the ingredients thoroughly until well blended. 3. Transfer the beef mixture into a lightly oiled baking pan, spreading it evenly. 4. Insert the baking pan into the air fryer, select the Bake setting, and cook the meatloaf for 25 minutes.

Herb-Roasted Beef with Carrots

Prep time: 10 minutes | Cook time: 55 minutes | Serves 5

- 2 pounds (907 g) top sirloin roast
- 2 tablespoons olive oil
- Sea salt and ground black pepper, to taste
- 2 carrots, sliced
- 1 tablespoon fresh coriander
- 1 tablespoon fresh thyme
- 1 tablespoon fresh rosemary

1. Preheat the air fryer to 390°F (199°C). 2. In a bowl, toss the beef with olive oil, salt, and black pepper until well coated, then place the beef in the crisper tray. 3. Insert the crisper tray into the air fryer, select the Roast setting, and cook the beef for 45 minutes, flipping it halfway through for even cooking. 4. After 45 minutes, add the carrots and herbs on top of the beef, then continue cooking for an additional 10 minutes. 5. Enjoy your meal!

Honey-Glazed Orange Ham

Prep time: 5 minutes | Cook time: 1 hour | Serves 4

- 1½ pounds (680 g) smoked and cooked ham
- ¼ cup honey
- 1 small-sized orange, freshly squeezed
- 1 tablespoon balsamic vinegar
- 1 tablespoon stone-ground mustard
- ½ teaspoon crushed red pepper flakes
- Freshly ground black pepper, to taste

1. Preheat the air fryer to 400°F (205°C). 2. In a mixing bowl, whisk together all the remaining ingredients to create the glaze. 3. Wrap the ham tightly in aluminum foil and place it in the crisper tray. Then, reduce the temperature to 375°F (190°C) and insert the crisper tray into the air fryer. Select the Air Fry setting and cook the ham for approximately 30 minutes. 4. After 30 minutes, carefully remove the foil, increase the temperature back to 400°F (205°C), and continue cooking for an additional 15 minutes, brushing the ham with the glaze every 5 minutes.

Shaoxing Wine-Infused Pork Chops

Prep time: 10 minutes | Cook time: 15 minutes | Serves 4

- 1½ pounds (680 g) pork loin porterhouse, cut into 4 slices
- 1½ tablespoons sesame oil
- ½ teaspoon five-spice powder
- 2 garlic cloves, crushed
- 1 tablespoon soy sauce
- 1 tablespoon hoisin sauce
- 2 tablespoons Shaoxing wine

1. Preheat the air fryer to 400°F (205°C). 2. Arrange all the ingredients in a lightly greased crisper tray. 3. Insert the crisper tray into the air fryer, select the Air Fry setting, and cook the pork loin chops for 15 minutes, flipping them halfway through for even cooking. 4. Enjoy your meal!

Lemon Fennel Pork Souvlaki

Prep time: 15 minutes | Cook time: 15 minutes | Serves 4

1 tablespoon olive oil	juiced
½ teaspoon sweet paprika	1 eggplant, diced
1 pound (454 g) pork tenderloin, cubed	2 bell peppers, diced
1 small lemon, freshly	½ pound (227 g) fennel, diced

1. Preheat the air fryer to 400°F (205°C). 2. In a mixing bowl, toss all the ingredients together until they are evenly coated on all sides. 3. Thread the coated ingredients onto skewers and arrange them in the crisper tray. 4. Insert the crisper tray into the air fryer, select the Air Fry setting, and cook the skewers for about 15 minutes, flipping them halfway through for even cooking.

Herb-Crusted Pork Roast

Prep time: 5 minutes | Cook time: 55 minutes | Serves 5

2 pounds (907 g) pork center cut	1 teaspoon crushed red pepper flakes
2 tablespoons olive oil	Sea salt and freshly ground black pepper, to taste
1 tablespoon Italian herb mix	

1. Preheat the air fryer to 360°F (182°C). 2. In a lightly greased crisper tray, toss all the ingredients together until evenly coated. 3. Insert the crisper tray into the air fryer, select the Air Fry setting, and cook the pork for 55 minutes, flipping it halfway through to ensure even cooking. 4. Serve warm and enjoy!

Crispy Cheese-Crusted Sirloin Chops

Prep time: 5 minutes | Cook time: 15 minutes | Serves 3

1 pound (454 g) sirloin chops	pepper, to taste
1 egg	3 tablespoons grated Pecorino cheese
2 tablespoons butter, at room temperature	½ cup bread crumbs
Sea salt and ground black	1 teaspoon paprika
	1 teaspoon garlic powder

1. Start by preheating the air fryer to 400°F (205°C). 2. Pat the pork sirloin chops dry with kitchen towels. 3. In a shallow bowl, whisk the egg until pale and frothy. 4. In another shallow bowl, thoroughly combine the remaining ingredients. Dip the pork chops into the egg, then the cheese and crumb mixture. 5. Place the pork sirloin chops in a lightly oiled crisper tray. 6. Place the crisper tray in the corresponding position in the air fryer. Select Air Fry and cook the pork sirloin chops for 15 minutes, turning them over halfway through the cooking time.

Herb-Roasted Sausage and Brussels Sprouts

Prep time: 5 minutes | Cook time: 15 minutes | Serves 4

1 pound (454 g) sausage links, uncooked	1 teaspoon dried rosemary
1 pound (454 g) Brussels sprouts, halved	1 teaspoon dried parsley flakes
1 teaspoon dried thyme	1 teaspoon garlic powder

1. Preheat the air fryer to 380°F (193°C). 2. Arrange the sausage and Brussels sprouts in a lightly greased crisper tray. 3. Insert the crisper tray into the air fryer, select the Air Fry setting, and cook the sausage and Brussels sprouts for about 15 minutes, tossing the contents halfway through for even cooking.

Spicy Teriyaki Pork Burgers

Prep time: 10 minutes | Cook time: 15 minutes | Serves 4

1 pound (454 g) ground pork	1 teaspoon sliced habanero pepper
Kosher salt and ground black pepper, to taste	1 tablespoon teriyaki sauce
1 tablespoon chopped fresh parsley	1 small onion, chopped
1 tablespoon chopped fresh coriander	1 clove garlic, minced
	4 brioche hamburger buns, lightly toasted

1. Preheat the air fryer to 380°F (193°C). 2. In a mixing bowl, combine the pork, spices, habanero pepper, teriyaki sauce, onion, and garlic until thoroughly mixed. Shape the mixture into four patties. 3. Place the patties in the crisper tray, ensuring they are spaced apart. 4. Insert the crisper tray into the air fryer, select the Air Fry setting, and cook the pork patties for about 15 minutes, flipping them halfway through to ensure they are cooked evenly. 5. Serve the patties on brioche hamburger buns. Enjoy your meal!

Santa Maria Rotisserie Tri-Tip Roast

Prep time: 10 minutes | Cook time: 1½ hours | Serves 8

- 2 tri-tip roasts (2 pounds / 907 g each)

Rub:

- 1½ tablespoons kosher salt
- 2 teaspoons freshly ground black pepper
- 1½ teaspoons sugar

- 1 teaspoon garlic powder
- ½ teaspoon ancho chile powder or 1 teaspoon chili powder

Baste:

- ⅓ cup water
- 1 tablespoon rub mixture

- 1 tablespoon white vinegar

1. Begin by preheating the air fryer to 400ºF (205ºC). 2. Prepare the rub by combining the rub ingredients in a small bowl, reserving 1 tablespoon of the mixture for later use. Apply the remaining rub evenly on both sides of the tri-tip roasts and let them sit for 10 to 15 minutes before threading them onto the rotisserie spit. 3. Next, prepare the baste by mixing the baste ingredients in a small bowl until well combined, then set aside. 4. Stack one tri-tip on top of the other, ensuring the small ends are on opposite sides. Fold in the ends and tie the roasts together with kitchen twine to form a single, uniform roast. Insert a long skewer through the center of the roast lengthwise to create a pilot hole, then run the rotisserie spit through the hole and secure it with the forks, adjusting for balance as necessary. 5. Place the roast on the preheated grill, setting a drip tray underneath and adding 1 to 2 cups of hot water to the tray. Select the Rotisserie setting and cook the roast for 80 to 90 minutes. In the last 30 minutes of cooking, begin basting with the reserved sauce, repeating this 6 to 8 times until the roast is well coated and the internal temperature reaches around 140ºF (60ºC). Be aware that the roast may shrink during cooking, so adjust the forks as needed. 6. Once done, carefully remove the rotisserie forks and slide the spit out. Place the roast on a large cutting board, cover it with aluminum foil, and let it rest for 15 minutes. Cut off the twine, separate the roasts, slice against the grain, and serve.

Herb–Crusted Filet Mignon with Basil

Prep time: 5 minutes | Cook time: 14 minutes | Serves 4

- 1½ pounds (680 g) filet mignon
- Sea salt and ground black pepper, to taste
- 2 tablespoons olive oil
- 1 teaspoon dried rosemary

- 1 teaspoon dried thyme
- 1 teaspoon dried basil
- 2 cloves garlic, minced

1. Preheat the air fryer to 400ºF (205ºC). 2. In a bowl, toss the beef with all the remaining ingredients until well coated, then place the beef in the crisper tray. 3. Insert the crisper tray into the air fryer, select the Air Fry setting, and cook the beef for 14 minutes, flipping it halfway through for even cooking. 4. Enjoy your meal!

Mustard Garlic Shredded Beef Brisket

Prep time: 5 minutes | Cook time: 1 hour | Serves 4

- 1½ pounds (680 g) beef brisket
- 2 tablespoons olive oil
- 3 garlic cloves, pressed
- Sea salt and ground black pepper, to taste
- 1 teaspoon crushed red pepper flakes
- 2 tablespoons tomato ketchup
- 2 tablespoons Dijon mustard

1. Begin by preheating your air fryer to 390°F (199°C) to get it ready for the brisket. 2. In a mixing bowl, coat the beef brisket with olive oil, minced garlic, salt, black pepper, and red pepper, ensuring an even distribution of flavors. Next, place the seasoned brisket in the crisper tray. 3. Insert the crisper tray into the appropriate slot in the air fryer. Choose the Roast setting and cook the beef brisket for 15 minutes. After this initial cooking time, flip the brisket over and reduce the temperature to 360°F (182°C). 4. Continue cooking the beef brisket for about 55 minutes, or until it is fully cooked through and tender. 5. Once cooked, use two forks to shred the beef. Mix in ketchup and mustard, stirring until everything is well combined for a flavorful finish. Enjoy your deliciously shredded brisket!

Cuban Pork and Cheese Sandwich

Prep time: 10 minutes | Cook time: 55 minutes | Serves 4

- 1½ pounds (680 g) pork butt
- 1 teaspoon stone-ground mustard
- ½ teaspoon ground cumin
- 2 cloves garlic, crushed
- Kosher salt and freshly ground black pepper, to taste
- ½ teaspoon ground allspice
- 2 tablespoons fresh pineapple juice
- 2 ounces (57 g) Swiss cheese, sliced
- 16 ounces (454 g) Cuban bread loaf, sliced

1. Start by preheating the air fryer to 360°F (182°C). 2. Toss all ingredients , except for the cheese and bread, in a lightly greased crisper tray. 3. Place the crisper tray in the corresponding position in the air fryer. Select Air Fry and cook the pork butt for 55 minutes, turning it over halfway through the cooking time. 4. Using two forks, shred the pork; assemble the sandwiches with cheese and bread. Serve warm and enjoy!

Chapter

5

Fish and Seafood

Chapter 5 Fish and Seafood

Cheesy Garlic Squid Tubes

Prep time: 6 minutes | Cook time: 5 minutes | Serves 4

- 1½ pounds (680 g) small squid tubes
- 2 tablespoons butter, melted
- 1 chili pepper, chopped
- 2 garlic cloves, minced
- 1 teaspoon red pepper flakes
- Sea salt and ground black pepper, to taste
- ¼ cup dry white wine
- 2 tablespoons fresh lemon juice
- 1 teaspoon Mediterranean herb mix
- 2 tablespoons grated Parmigiano-Reggiano cheese

1. Begin by preheating your air fryer to a hot 400ºF (205ºC) to prepare for cooking. 2. In a lightly greased crisper tray, combine all the ingredients except for the Parmigiano-Reggiano cheese, tossing them well to ensure even coverage. 3. Insert the crisper tray into its designated position in the air fryer. Choose the Air Fry setting and cook the squid for 5 minutes, making sure to toss the crisper tray halfway through for an even cook. 4. Once finished, sprinkle the warm squid with the Parmigiano-Reggiano cheese for a deliciously cheesy touch!

Crispy Panko-Crusted Salmon Strips

Prep time: 5 minutes | Cook time: 10 minutes | Serves 4

- 1 egg, beaten
- ½ cup all-purpose flour
- Sea salt and ground black pepper, to taste
- 1 teaspoon hot paprika
- ½ cup seasoned bread crumbs
- 1 tablespoon olive oil
- 1 pound (454 g) salmon strips

1. Start by preheating the air fryer to 400ºF (205ºC). 2. In a mixing bowl, thoroughly combine the egg, flour, and spices. In a separate bowl, thoroughly combine the bread crumbs and olive oil. 3. Now, dip the salmon strips into the flour mixture to coat; roll the fish pieces over the bread crumb mixture until they are well coated on all sides. 4. Arrange the salmon strips in the crisper tray. 5. Place the crisper tray in the corresponding position in the air fryer. Select Air Fry and cook the salmon strips for 10 minutes, turning them over halfway through the cooking time.

Spicy Mackerel Patties on English Muffins

Prep time: 10 minutes | Cook time: 14 minutes | Serves 4

- 1 pound (454 g) mackerel fillet, boneless and chopped
- 1 tablespoon olive oil
- ½ onion, chopped
- 2 garlic cloves, crushed
- 1 teaspoon hot paprika
- 1 tablespoon chopped fresh cilantro
- 2 tablespoons chopped fresh parsley
- Sea salt and ground black pepper, to taste
- 4 English muffins, toasted

1. Start by preheating the air fryer to 400ºF (205ºC). 2. Mix all ingredients , except for the English muffins, in a bowl. Shape the mixture into four patties and place them in a lightly oiled crisper tray. 3. Place the crisper tray in the corresponding position in the air fryer. Select Air Fry and cook the fish patties for about 14 minutes, turning them over halfway through the cooking time. 4. Serve on English muffins and enjoy!

Spicy Cayenne Shrimp

Prep time: 10 minutes | Cook time: 6 minutes | Serves 4

- 1½ pounds (680 g) raw shrimp, peeled and deveined
- 1 tablespoon olive oil
- 1 teaspoon minced garlic
- 1 teaspoon cayenne pepper
- ½ teaspoon lemon pepper
- Sea salt, to taste

1. Preheat the air fryer to 400ºF (205ºC). 2. In a lightly greased crisper tray, toss all the ingredients together until evenly coated. 3. Insert the crisper tray into the air fryer, select the Air Fry setting, and cook the shrimp for 6 minutes, tossing the contents halfway through for even cooking.

Crispy Buttermilk Shrimp

Prep time: 10 minutes | Cook time: 10 minutes | Serves 4

1 cup all-purpose flour	½ cup buttermilk
1 teaspoon Old Bay seasoning	1 cup seasoned bread crumbs
Sea salt and lemon pepper, to taste	1½ pounds (680 g) shrimp, peeled and deveined

1. Start by preheating the air fryer to 400ºF (205ºC). 2. In a shallow bowl, mix the flour, spices, and buttermilk. Place the seasoned bread crumbs in the second bowl. 3. Dip the shrimp in the flour mixture, then in the bread crumbs until they are well coated on all sides. 4. Arrange the shrimp in a greased crisper tray. 5. Place the crisper tray in the corresponding position in the air fryer. Select Air Fry and cook the shrimp for about 10 minutes, shaking crisper tray halfway through the cooking time.

Herb Butter Jumbo Shrimp

Prep time: 6 minutes | Cook time: 8 minutes | Serves 4

1 pound (454 g) jumbo shrimp	2 tablespoons chopped fresh cilantro
2 tablespoons butter, room temperature	2 tablespoons chopped fresh chives
Coarse sea salt and lemon pepper, to taste	2 garlic cloves, crushed

1. Start by preheating the air fryer to 400ºF (205ºC). 2. Toss all ingredients in a lightly greased crisper tray. 3. Place the crisper tray in the corresponding position in the air fryer. Select Air Fry and cook the shrimp for 8 minutes, tossing crisper tray halfway through the cooking time.

Parmesan-Crusted Monkfish Fillets

Prep time: 5 minutes | Cook time: 14 minutes | Serves 4

1 pound (454 g) monkfish fillets	2 tablespoons butter
Coarse sea salt and ground black pepper, to taste	2 tablespoons lemon juice
	4 tablespoon grated Parmesan cheese

1. Begin by preheating your air fryer to a scorching 400ºF (205ºC) to prepare for cooking. 2. In a mixing bowl, toss the fish fillets with all the remaining ingredients except for the Parmesan cheese. Once well-coated, place the fillets in a lightly oiled crisper tray to prevent sticking. 3. Insert the crisper tray into its designated position in the air fryer. Choose the Air Fry setting and cook the fish fillets for about 14 minutes, flipping them over halfway through to ensure even cooking. 4. After cooking, sprinkle the grated Parmesan cheese over the hot fish fillets and serve immediately for a deliciously cheesy finish!

Crispy Cheesy Monkfish Strips

Prep time: 10 minutes | Cook time: 10 minutes | Serves 4

½ cup all-purpose flour	1 teaspoon garlic powder
Sea salt and ground black pepper, to taste	1 egg, whisked
1 teaspoon cayenne pepper	½ cup grated Pecorino Romano cheese
½ teaspoon onion powder	1 pound (454 g) monkfish, sliced into strips
1 tablespoon chopped Italian parsley	

1. Begin by preheating your air fryer to a high 400ºF (205ºC) to create the perfect cooking environment. 2. In a shallow bowl, combine the flour, spices, egg, and cheese to form a batter. Dip each fish strip into the batter, ensuring they are thoroughly coated on all sides. 3. Once coated, arrange the fish strips neatly in the crisper tray for even cooking. 4. Insert the crisper tray into its designated position in the air fryer. Select the Air Fry setting and cook the fish strips for about 10 minutes, shaking the crisper tray halfway through to ensure they cook evenly. Enjoy your crispy fish strips!

Herb-Infused Butter Sea Bass

Prep time: 5 minutes | Cook time: 10 minutes | Serves 3

2 tablespoons butter, room temperature	Sea salt and ground black pepper, to taste
1 pound (454 g) sea bass	1 teaspoon mustard seeds
¼ cup dry white wine	1 teaspoon fennel seeds
¼ cup all-purpose flour	2 cloves garlic, minced

1. Start by preheating the air fryer to 400ºF (205ºC). 2. Toss the fish with the remaining ingredients; place them in a lightly oiled crisper tray. 3. Place the crisper tray in the corresponding position in the air fryer. Select Air Fry and cook the fish for about 10 minutes, turning them over halfway through the cooking time.

Garlic-Seasoned Sea Bass

Prep time: 5 minutes | Cook time: 10 minutes | Serves 4

- 1 pound (454 g) sea bass
- 2 garlic cloves, minced
- 2 tablespoons olive oil
- 1 tablespoon Italian
- seasoning mix
- Sea salt and ground black pepper, to taste
- ¼ cup dry white wine

1. Start by preheating the air fryer to 400ºF (205ºC). 2. Toss the fish with the remaining ingredients; place them in a lightly oiled crisper tray. 3. Place the crisper tray in the corresponding position in the air fryer. Select Air Fry and cook the fish for about 10 minutes, turning them over halfway through the cooking time.

Crispy Coconut Shrimp

Prep time: 10 minutes | Cook time: 9 minutes | Serves 4

- ½ cup whole wheat flour
- 1 cup shredded coconut
- ¼ cup buttermilk
- 2 tablespoons olive oil
- 2 garlic cloves, crushed
- 1 tablespoon fresh lemon juice
- Sea salt and red pepper flakes, to taste
- 1½ pounds (680 g) shrimp, peeled and deveined

1. Start by preheating the air fryer to 400ºF (205ºC). 2. Mix the flour, coconut, buttermilk, olive oil, garlic, lemon juice, salt, and red pepper in a mixing bowl. 3. Dip the shrimp in the batter and place them in a greased crisper tray. 4. Place the crisper tray in the corresponding position in the air fryer. Select Air Fry and cook the shrimp for 9 minutes, tossing crisper tray halfway through the cooking time.

Herbed Lemon Salmon Fillets

Prep time: 6 minutes | Cook time: 12 minutes | Serves 4

- 1½ pounds (680 g) salmon fillets
- 2 sprigs fresh rosemary
- 1 tablespoon fresh basil
- 1 tablespoon fresh thyme
- 1 tablespoon fresh dill
- 1 small lemon, juiced
- 2 tablespoons olive oil
- Sea salt and ground black pepper, to taste
- 1 teaspoon stone-ground mustard
- 2 cloves garlic, chopped

1. First, preheat your air fryer to 380ºF (193ºC) to get it ready for cooking. 2. In a bowl, toss the salmon with the remaining ingredients until well coated, then place the fillets in a lightly oiled crisper tray to prevent sticking. 3. Insert the crisper tray into its designated position in the air fryer. Select the Roast setting and cook the salmon fillets for approximately 12 minutes, flipping them over halfway through to ensure even cooking. 4. Once done, serve immediately and enjoy the delicious flavors of your perfectly cooked salmon!

Garlic-Infused Swordfish Steaks

Prep time: 5 minutes | Cook time: 10 minutes | Serves 4

- 1 pound (454 g) swordfish steaks
- 4 garlic cloves, peeled
- 4 tablespoons olive oil
- 2 tablespoons fresh lemon juice
- 1 tablespoon roughly chopped fresh cilantro
- 1 teaspoon Spanish paprika
- Sea salt and ground black pepper, to taste

1. Start by preheating the air fryer to 400ºF (205ºC). 2. Toss the swordfish steaks with the remaining ingredients and place them in a lightly oiled crisper tray. 3. Place the crisper tray in the corresponding position in the air fryer. Select Air Fry and cook the swordfish steaks for about 10 minutes, turning them over halfway through the cooking time.

Spicy Lemon Prawns with Garlic

Prep time: 15 minutes | Cook time: 9 minutes | Serves 4

- 1½ pounds (680 g) prawns, peeled and deveined
- 2 garlic cloves, minced
- 2 tablespoons chopped fresh chives
- ½ cup whole-wheat flour
- ½ teaspoon sweet paprika
- 1 teaspoon hot paprika
- Salt and freshly ground black pepper, to taste
- 2 tablespoons coconut oil
- 2 tablespoons lemon juice

1. Begin by preheating your air fryer to a hot 400ºF (205ºC) to prepare for the prawns. 2. In a lightly greased crisper tray, combine all the ingredients, tossing them together to ensure they are evenly coated. 3. Insert the crisper tray into its designated position in the air fryer. Select the Air Fry setting and cook the prawns for 9 minutes, making sure to toss the crisper tray halfway through for even cooking. Enjoy your perfectly cooked prawns!

Garlic Butter Halibut Steaks

Prep time: 5 minutes | Cook time: 12 minutes | Serves 4

1 pound (454 g) halibut steaks	2 tablespoons chopped fresh chives
¼ cup butter	1 teaspoon minced garlic
Sea salt, to taste	1 teaspoon ground mixed peppercorns

1. Preheat the air fryer to 400ºF (205ºC). 2. In a bowl, toss the halibut steaks with all the remaining ingredients until well coated, then place them in a lightly oiled crisper tray. 3. Insert the crisper tray into the air fryer, select the Air Fry setting, and cook the halibut steaks for approximately 12 minutes, flipping them halfway through for even cooking.

Lemon-Spiced Calamari Rings

Prep time: 10 minutes | Cook time: 5 minutes | Serves 4

1 pound (454 g) calamari, sliced into rings	1 teaspoon cayenne pepper
Sea salt and ground black pepper, to taste	1 teaspoon garlic powder
	2 tablespoons lemon juice
	2 tablespoons olive oil

1. Begin by preheating your air fryer to a sizzling 400ºF (205ºC) to prepare for cooking. 2. In a lightly greased crisper tray, combine all the ingredients, tossing them together to ensure even coverage. 3. Insert the crisper tray into the designated position in the air fryer. Select the Air Fry setting and cook the calamari for 5 minutes, tossing the crisper tray halfway through for consistent cooking. Enjoy your deliciously cooked calamari!

Paprika and Parsley Squid Tubes

Prep time: 5 minutes | Cook time: 5 minutes | Serves 4

1½ pounds (680 g) small squid tubes	1 teaspoon paprika
Sea salt and ground black pepper, to taste	½ cup minced parsley
	2 cloves garlic, minced
	¼ cup olive oil

1. Begin by preheating your air fryer to a hot 400ºF (205ºC) to prepare for cooking. 2. In a lightly greased crisper tray, toss the squid together with salt, black pepper, and paprika, ensuring everything is well coated. 3. Insert the crisper tray into its designated position in the air fryer. Select the Air Fry setting and cook the squid for 5 minutes, tossing the tray halfway through for even cooking. Enjoy your perfectly cooked squid!

Creamy Prawn Salad with Dill

Prep time: 10 minutes | Cook time: 6 minutes | Serves 4

1½ pounds (680 g) king prawns, peeled and deveined	1 cup mayonnaise
Coarse sea salt and ground black pepper, to taste	1 teaspoon Dijon mustard
	1 tablespoon roughly chopped fresh parsley
1 tablespoon fresh lemon juice	1 teaspoon minced fresh dill
	1 shallot, chopped

1. Start by preheating the air fryer to 400ºF (205ºC). 2. Toss the prawns with the salt and black pepper in a lightly greased crisper tray. 3. Place the crisper tray in the corresponding position in the air fryer. Select Air Fry and cook the prawns for 6 minutes, tossing crisper tray halfway through the cooking time. 4. Add the prawns to a salad bowl; add in the remaining ingredients and stir to combine well.

Herbed Butter Mahi-Mahi Fillets

Prep time: 5 minutes | Cook time: 14 minutes | Serves 4

1 pound (454 g) mahi-mahi fillets	ground black pepper, to taste
2 tablespoons butter, room temperature	1 teaspoon smoked paprika
2 tablespoons fresh lemon juice	1 teaspoon minced garlic
	1 teaspoon dried basil
Kosher salt and freshly	1 teaspoon dried oregano

1. Start by preheating the air fryer to 400ºF (205ºC). 2. Toss the fish fillets with the remaining ingredients and place them in a lightly oiled crisper tray. 3. Place the crisper tray in the corresponding position in the air fryer. Select Air Fry and cook the fish fillets for about 14 minutes, turning them over halfway through the cooking time.

Crispy Beer-Battered Calamari Rings

Prep time: 5 minutes | Cook time: 5 minutes | Serves 4

- 2 cups all-purpose flour
- 1 cup beer
- Sea salt and ground black pepper, to taste
- 2 teaspoons garlic powder
- 1 teaspoon dried parsley flakes
- 1 tablespoon olive oil
- 1 pound (454 g) calamari rings

1. Preheat the air fryer to 400°F (205°C). 2. In a mixing bowl, combine the flour, beer, spices, and olive oil until well mixed. 3. Dip each piece of calamari into the flour mixture to coat thoroughly, then arrange the coated calamari in the crisper tray. 4. Insert the crisper tray into the air fryer, select the Air Fry setting, and cook the calamari for 5 minutes, flipping them halfway through for even cooking.

Garlic Butter Calamari

Prep time: 10 minutes | Cook time: 5 minutes | Serves 4

- 1 pound (454 g) calamari, sliced into rings
- 2 tablespoons butter, melted
- 4 garlic cloves, smashed
- 2 tablespoons sherry wine
- 2 tablespoons fresh lemon juice
- Coarse sea salt and ground black pepper, to taste
- 1 teaspoon paprika
- 1 teaspoon dried oregano

1. Preheat the air fryer to 400°F (205°C). 2. In a lightly greased crisper tray, toss all the ingredients together until well combined. 3. Insert the crisper tray into the air fryer, select the Air Fry setting, and cook the calamari for 5 minutes, tossing the tray halfway through for even cooking.

Mediterranean Mackerel Pitas with Feta

Prep time: 5 minutes | Cook time: 14 minutes | Serves 4

- 1 pound (454 g) mackerel fish fillets
- 2 tablespoons olive oil
- 1 tablespoon Mediterranean seasoning mix
- ½ teaspoon chili powder
- Sea salt and freshly ground black pepper, to taste
- 2 ounces (57 g) feta cheese, crumbled
- 4 tortillas

1. Preheat the air fryer to 400°F (205°C). 2. In a bowl, toss the fish fillets with olive oil until evenly coated, then arrange them in a lightly oiled crisper tray. 3. Insert the crisper tray into the air fryer, select the Air Fry setting, and cook the fish fillets for about 14 minutes, flipping them halfway through for even cooking. 4. Once cooked, assemble the pitas with the chopped fish and any remaining ingredients, and serve warm.

Herb-Crusted Tilapia Nuggets

Prep time: 10 minutes | Cook time: 10 minutes | Serves 4

- 1½ pounds (680 g) tilapia fillets, cut into 1½-inch pieces
- 1 tablespoon dried thyme
- 1 tablespoon dried oregano
- 1 tablespoon Dijon mustard
- 2 tablespoons olive oil
- 1½ cups all-purpose flour
- Sea salt and ground black pepper, to taste
- ½ teaspoon baking powder

1. Preheat the air fryer to 400°F (205°C). 2. Use kitchen towels to pat the fish dry. 3. In a mixing bowl, combine all the remaining ingredients until well mixed. Dip the fish pieces into the batter, ensuring they are thoroughly coated. 4. Arrange the coated fish in the crisper tray. 5. Insert the crisper tray into the air fryer, select the Air Fry setting, and cook the fish nuggets for 10 minutes, shaking the crisper tray halfway through for even cooking.

Lemon Garlic Squid

Prep time: 15 minutes | Cook time: 5 minutes | Serves 5

- 1½ pounds (680 g) squid, cut into pieces
- 1 chili pepper, chopped
- 1 small lemon, squeezed
- 2 tablespoons olive oil
- 1 tablespoon capers, drained
- 2 garlic cloves, minced
- 1 tablespoon chopped coriander
- 2 tablespoons chopped parsley
- 1 teaspoon sweet paprika
- Sea salt and ground black pepper, to taste

1. Preheat the air fryer to 400°F (205°C). 2. In a lightly greased crisper tray, toss all the ingredients together until evenly coated. 3. Insert the crisper tray into the air fryer, select the Air Fry setting, and cook the squid for 5 minutes, tossing the tray halfway through for even cooking.

Savory Sausage-Stuffed Squid

Prep time: 10 minutes | Cook time: 5 minutes | Serves 4

- 2 tablespoons olive oil, divided, plus more as needed
- 1 small onion, chopped
- 2 cloves garlic, minced
- 1 tablespoon chopped fresh parsley
- 1 small Italian pepper, chopped
- Sea salt and ground black pepper, to taste
- 4 ounces (113 g) beef sausage, crumbled
- 1 pound (454 g) squid tubes, cleaned

1. Begin by preheating your air fryer to a high 400°F (205°C) to prepare for cooking. 2. In a mixing bowl, combine the olive oil, onion, garlic, parsley, Italian pepper, salt, black pepper, and sausage until everything is well blended. 3. Carefully stuff the squid tubes with the sausage mixture and secure the openings with toothpicks to keep the filling intact. Arrange the stuffed squid in a lightly oiled crisper tray to prevent sticking. 4. Insert the crisper tray into the designated position in the air fryer. Select the Air Fry setting and cook the stuffed squid tubes for 5 minutes, turning them over halfway through to ensure even cooking. Enjoy your delicious stuffed squid!

Crispy Breaded Shrimp

Prep time: 10 minutes | Cook time: 10 minutes | Serves 4

- ½ cup flour
- Sea salt and lemon pepper, to taste
- 2 large eggs
- 1 cup seasoned bread crumbs
- 2 tablespoons olive oil
- 1 pound (454 g) shrimp, peeled and deveined

1. Begin by preheating your air fryer to an impressive 400°F (205°C) to set the stage for your shrimp. 2. In a shallow bowl, combine the flour, salt, and lemon pepper to create a dry mixture. In a second bowl, beat the eggs until well mixed, and in a third bowl, place the bread crumbs for coating. 3. Take each shrimp and dip it into the flour mixture, ensuring it's well coated. Next, immerse it in the beaten eggs, and finally, roll the shrimp in the bread crumbs until they are fully covered on all sides. 4. Arrange the breaded shrimp neatly in the crisper tray and drizzle olive oil over the top to enhance flavor and crispiness. 5. Insert the crisper tray into the designated position in the air fryer. Select the Air Fry setting and cook the shrimp for about 10 minutes, shaking the crisper tray halfway through to ensure even cooking. Enjoy your perfectly crispy shrimp!

Rosemary-Infused Swordfish Steaks

Prep time: 5 minutes | Cook time: 10 minutes | Serves 4

- 1 pound (454 g) swordfish steaks
- 2 tablespoons olive oil
- 2 teaspoons tamari sauce
- Salt and freshly ground pepper, to taste
- ¼ cup dry red wine
- 2 sprigs rosemary
- 1 sprig thyme
- 1 tablespoon grated lemon rind

1. Begin by marinating the swordfish steaks: toss them with the remaining ingredients in a ceramic dish, cover it, and let it sit in the refrigerator for about 2 hours to absorb all the flavors. 2. Once marinated, preheat your air fryer to a hot 400°F (205°C) to prepare for cooking. 3. After the marinating time, discard the marinade and place the fish in a lightly oiled crisper tray to prevent sticking. 4. Insert the crisper tray into its designated position in the air fryer. Select the Air Fry setting and cook the swordfish steaks for approximately 10 minutes, flipping them halfway through for even cooking. Enjoy your perfectly cooked swordfish!

Garlic Butter Lobster Tails

Prep time: 5 minutes | Cook time: 8 minutes | Serves 4

- 1 pound (454 g) lobster tails
- 4 tablespoons butter, room temperature
- 2 garlic cloves, minced
- Coarse sea salt and freshly cracked black pepper, to taste
- 4 tablespoons spring onions
- 1 tablespoon fresh lime juice

1. Preheat the air fryer to 380ºF (193ºC). 2. Butterfly the lobster tails by cutting through the shell and arrange them in a lightly oiled crisper tray. 3. In a mixing bowl, combine the remaining ingredients thoroughly. 4. Spread half of the butter mixture over the top of the lobster meat, then place the crisper tray into the air fryer. Select the Air Fry setting and cook the lobster tails for 4 minutes. 5. After 4 minutes, spread the remaining butter mixture on top and continue cooking for an additional 4 minutes.

Crispy Buttermilk Tilapia Strips

Prep time: 10 minutes | Cook time: 10 minutes | Serves 4

- ½ cup all-purpose flour
- 1 large egg
- 2 tablespoons buttermilk
- ½ cup crushed crackers
- 1 teaspoon garlic powder
- Sea salt and ground black pepper, to taste
- ½ teaspoon cayenne pepper
- 1 pound (454 g) tilapia fillets, cut into strips

1. Preheat the air fryer to 400ºF (205ºC). 2. In a shallow bowl, add the flour. In a second bowl, whisk together the egg and buttermilk. In a third bowl, mix the crushed crackers with the spices. 3. Dip the fish strips first in the flour mixture, then in the whisked egg mixture, and finally roll them in the cracker mixture until fully coated on all sides. 4. Arrange the coated fish sticks in the crisper tray. 5. Insert the crisper tray into the air fryer, select the Air Fry setting, and cook the fish sticks for about 10 minutes, shaking the tray halfway through for even cooking.

Garlic Rosemary Sea Scallops

Prep time: 5 minutes | Cook time: 7 minutes | Serves 4

- 1½ pounds (680 g) sea scallops
- 4 tablespoons butter, melted
- 1 tablespoon minced garlic
- Sea salt and ground black pepper, to taste
- 2 rosemary sprigs, leaves picked and chopped
- 4 tablespoons dry white wine

1. Preheat the air fryer to 400ºF (205ºC). 2. In a lightly greased crisper tray, toss all the ingredients together until well combined. 3. Insert the crisper tray into the air fryer, select the Air Fry setting, and cook the scallops for 7 minutes, tossing the tray halfway through for even cooking.

Chapter
6

Snacks and Appetizers

Chapter 6 Snacks and Appetizers

Cinnamon Apple Cream Cheese Rolls

Prep time: 10 minutes | Cook time: 10 minutes | Serves 4

- 6 ounces (170 g) refrigerated crescent rolls
- 1 apple, peeled, cored, and grated
- 6 ounces (170 g) cream cheese, crumbled
- ¼ cup brown sugar
- 1 teaspoon apple pie spice

1. Start by preheating the air fryer to 320ºF (160ºC). 2. Separate the dough into rectangles. Mix the remaining ingredients until well combined. 3. Spread each rectangle with the cheese mixture; roll them up tightly. Place the rolls in the baking pan. 4. Place the baking pan in the corresponding position in the air fryer. Select Bake and cook the rolls for about 5 minutes; turn them over and bake for a further 5 minutes.

Spicy Chili Cauliflower Bites

Prep time: 5 minutes | Cook time: 15 minutes | Serves 4

- 2 eggs, whisked
- 1 cup bread crumbs
- Sea salt and ground black pepper, to taste
- 1 teaspoon cayenne pepper
- 1 teaspoon chili powder
- ½ teaspoon onion powder
- ½ teaspoon cumin powder
- ½ teaspoon garlic powder
- 1 pound (454 g) cauliflower florets

1. Begin by preheating your air fryer to 350ºF (180ºC) to prepare for cooking. 2. In a mixing bowl, combine the eggs, bread crumbs, and spices until the mixture is well blended. Dip each cauliflower floret into the batter, ensuring they are thoroughly coated. Transfer the coated florets to the crisper tray. 3. Insert the crisper tray into its designated position in the air fryer. Select the Air Fry setting and cook the cauliflower florets for approximately 15 minutes, turning them over halfway through to achieve even crispiness. Enjoy your tasty, golden-brown cauliflower!

Crispy Paprika Potato Chips

Prep time: 10 minutes | Cook time: 16 minutes | Serves 3

- 1 pound (454 g) potatoes, thinly sliced
- 2 tablespoons olive oil
- 1 teaspoon paprika
- Coarse salt and cayenne pepper, to taste

1. First, preheat your air fryer to 360ºF (182ºC) to get it ready for the potatoes. 2. In a mixing bowl, toss the potatoes with the remaining ingredients, ensuring they are evenly coated. Then, place the seasoned potatoes in the crisper tray. 3. Insert the crisper tray into its designated position in the air fryer. Select the Air Fry setting and cook the potato chips for 16 minutes, shaking the crisper tray halfway through the cooking time. If necessary, work in batches to avoid overcrowding. 4. Once cooked, enjoy your delicious, crispy potato chips!

Sweet and Savory Chicken Wings

Prep time: 6 minutes | Cook time: 18 minutes | Serves 5

- 2 pounds (907 g) chicken wings
- ¼ cup agave syrup
- 2 tablespoons soy sauce
- 2 tablespoons chopped scallions
- 2 tablespoons olive oil
- 1 teaspoon peeled and grated ginger
- 2 cloves garlic, minced
- Sea salt and ground black pepper, to taste

1. Begin by preheating your air fryer to 380ºF (193ºC) to prepare for cooking. 2. In a mixing bowl, toss the chicken wings with the remaining ingredients until they are well coated. Transfer the seasoned wings to the crisper tray. 3. Insert the crisper tray into its designated position in the air fryer. Select the Roast setting and cook the chicken wings for 18 minutes, turning them over halfway through to ensure even cooking and crispiness. Enjoy your deliciously roasted chicken wings!

Crispy Air-Fried Mixed Nuts

Prep time: 2 minutes | Cook time: 6 minutes | Serves 4

- ¼ cup almonds
- ½ cup hazelnuts
- ¼ cup peanuts

1. Start by preheating the air fryer to 330ºF (166ºC). 2. Place the nuts in the crisper tray. 3. Place the crisper tray in the corresponding position in the air fryer. Select Air Fry and cook the nuts for 6 minutes, shaking the crisper tray halfway through the cooking time and working in batches. 4. Enjoy!

Paprika-Spiced Carrot Bites

Prep time: 10 minutes | Cook time: 15 minutes | Serves 4

- 1 pound (454 g) carrots, cut into slices
- 2 tablespoons coconut oil
- 1 teaspoon paprika
- ½ teaspoon garlic powder
- ½ teaspoon dried oregano
- ½ teaspoon dried parsley flakes
- Sea salt and ground black pepper, to taste

1. Preheat the air fryer to 380ºF (193ºC). 2. In a bowl, toss the carrots with the remaining ingredients until well coated, then arrange them in the crisper tray. 3. Insert the crisper tray into the air fryer, select the Air Fry setting, and cook the carrots for 15 minutes, shaking the tray halfway through for even cooking.

Cheesy Garlic Brussels Sprouts

Prep time: 10 minutes | Cook time: 10 minutes | Serves 4

- 1 pound (454 g) Brussels sprouts, trimmed
- 2 tablespoons butter, melted
- Sea salt and freshly ground black pepper, to taste
- 1 teaspoon minced garlic
- 2 tablespoons red wine vinegar
- 2 ounces (57 g) Cheddar cheese, shredded

1. Preheat the air fryer to 380ºF (193ºC). 2. In a bowl, toss the Brussels sprouts with the remaining ingredients until evenly coated, then arrange them in the crisper tray. 3. Insert the crisper tray into the air fryer, select the Air Fry setting, and cook the Brussels sprouts for 10 minutes, shaking the tray halfway through for even cooking. 4. Serve warm and enjoy your dish!

Cumin-Seasoned Wax Beans

Prep time: 6 minutes | Cook time: 6 minutes | Serves 4

- 1 pound (454 g) fresh wax beans, trimmed
- 2 teaspoons olive oil
- ½ teaspoon onion powder
- 1 teaspoon garlic powder
- ½ teaspoon cumin powder
- Sea salt and ground black pepper, to taste

1. Start by preheating the air fryer to 390ºF (199ºC). 2. Toss the wax beans with the remaining ingredients. Transfer to the crisper tray. 3. Place the crisper tray in the corresponding position in the air fryer. Select Air Fry and cook the wax beans for about 6 minutes, tossing the crisper tray halfway through the cooking time. 4. Enjoy!

Herbed Air-Fried Potato Chips

Prep time: 10 minutes | Cook time: 16 minutes | Serves 3

- 2 large-sized potatoes, thinly sliced
- 2 tablespoons olive oil
- 1 teaspoon Mediterranean
- herb mix
- 1 teaspoon cayenne pepper
- Coarse sea salt and ground black pepper, to taste

1. Start by preheating the air fryer to 360ºF (182ºC). 2. Toss the potatoes with the remaining ingredients and place them in the crisper tray. 3. Place the crisper tray in the corresponding position in the air fryer. Select Air Fry and cook the potato chips for 16 minutes, shaking the crisper tray halfway through the cooking time and working in batches. 4. Enjoy!

Spicy Mustard Chicken Wings

Prep time: 5 minutes | Cook time: 18 minutes | Serves 3

- ¾ pound (340 g) chicken wings
- 1 tablespoon olive oil
- 1 teaspoon mustard seeds
- 1 teaspoon cayenne pepper
- 1 teaspoon garlic powder
- Sea salt and ground black pepper, to taste

1. Start by preheating the air fryer to 380ºF (193ºC). 2. Toss the chicken wings with the remaining ingredients. Transfer to the crisper tray. 3. Place the crisper tray in the corresponding position in the air fryer. Select Roast and cook the chicken wings for 18 minutes, turning them over halfway through the cooking time.

Tangy Vinegar Chicken Drumettes

Prep time: 5 minutes | Cook time: 18 minutes | Serves 4

- 1 pound (454 g) chicken drumettes
- 4 tablespoons soy sauce
- ¼ cup rice vinegar
- 4 tablespoons honey
- 2 tablespoons sesame oil
- 1 teaspoon Gochugaru, Korean chili powder
- 2 tablespoons chopped scallions
- 2 garlic cloves, minced

1. Start by preheating the air fryer to 380ºF (193ºC). 2. Toss the chicken drumettes with the remaining ingredients. Transfer to the crisper tray. 3. Place the crisper tray in the corresponding position in the air fryer. Select Roast and cook the chicken drumettes for 18 minutes, turning them over halfway through the cooking time.

Maple Glazed Pancetta-Wrapped Shrimp

Prep time: 12 minutes | Cook time: 6 minutes | Serves 4

- 12 shrimp, peeled and deveined
- 3 slices pancetta, cut into
- strips
- 2 tablespoons maple syrup
- 1 tablespoon Dijon mustard

1. Begin by preheating your air fryer to a high 400ºF (205ºC) to prepare for cooking. 2. Take the shrimp and wrap each piece in pancetta strips, then toss them together with maple syrup and mustard for a delightful glaze. 3. Arrange the wrapped shrimp in a lightly greased crisper tray to prevent sticking. 4. Insert the crisper tray into its designated position in the air fryer. Select the Air Fry setting and cook the shrimp for 6 minutes, making sure to toss the crisper tray halfway through to ensure even cooking. Enjoy your deliciously sweet and savory shrimp!

Cinnamon-Spiced Apple Chips

Prep time: 10 minutes | Cook time: 9 minutes | Serves 4

- 2 large sweet, crisp apples, cored and sliced
- 1 teaspoon ground
- cinnamon
- ½ teaspoon grated nutmeg
- A pinch of salt

1. Begin by preheating your air fryer to a crisp 390ºF (199ºC) to prepare for cooking. 2. In a mixing bowl, toss the apple slices with the remaining ingredients until they are well coated. Arrange the slices in a single layer in the crisper tray to ensure even cooking. 3. Insert the crisper tray into its designated position in the air fryer. Select the Air Fry setting and cook the apple chips for approximately 9 minutes, shaking the crisper tray halfway through to promote uniform crispness. If needed, work in batches to prevent overcrowding. 4. Once done, enjoy your homemade apple chips for a delightful snack!

Spiced Peppercorn Potato Chips

Prep time: 10 minutes | Cook time: 16 minutes | Serves 3

- 2 large-sized potatoes, peeled and thinly sliced
- 2 tablespoons olive oil
- 1 teaspoon Sichuan peppercorns
- 1 teaspoon garlic powder
- ½ teaspoon Chinese five-spice powder
- Sea salt, to taste

1. First, preheat your air fryer to 360ºF (182ºC) to get it ready for the potatoes. 2. In a mixing bowl, combine the potatoes with the remaining ingredients, tossing them well to ensure even coating. Transfer the seasoned potatoes to the crisper tray. 3. Insert the crisper tray into its designated position in the air fryer. Select the Air Fry setting and cook the potato chips for 16 minutes, making sure to shake the crisper tray halfway through the cooking time. If needed, work in batches to prevent overcrowding. 4. Once cooked, enjoy your crispy and delicious potato chips!

Herbed Sweet Potato Chips

Prep time: 10 minutes | Cook time: 14 minutes | Serves 3

- 2 large-sized sweet potatoes, peeled and cut into thin slices
- 2 teaspoons butter, melted
- Sea salt and ground black
- pepper, to taste
- ½ teaspoon dried oregano
- ½ teaspoon dried basil
- ½ teaspoon dried rosemary

1. Start by preheating the air fryer to 360ºF (182ºC). 2. Toss the sweet potato with the remaining ingredients and place them in the crisper tray. 3. Place the crisper tray in the corresponding position in the air fryer. Select Air Fry and cook the sweet potato chips for 14 minutes, tossing halfway through the cooking time and working in batches. 4. Enjoy!

Mustard Mini Hot Dog Rolls

Prep time: 5 minutes | Cook time: 8 minutes | Serves 6

- 6 ounces (170 g) refrigerated crescent rolls
- 10 ounces (283 g) mini hot dogs
- 1 tablespoon mustard

1. Preheat the air fryer to 320ºF (160ºC). 2. Divide the dough into triangles and cut each triangle lengthwise into 3 smaller triangles. Spread mustard on each triangle. 3. Position a mini hot dog at the shortest side of each triangle and roll it up tightly. 4. Arrange the rolled-up hot dogs in a baking pan. 5. Insert the baking pan into the air fryer, select the Bake setting, and cook the rolls for approximately 8 minutes, flipping them halfway through for even cooking.

Zesty Lime Tortilla Chips

Prep time: 8 minutes | Cook time: 5 minutes | Serves 4

- 4 corn tortillas, cut into wedges
- 1 tablespoon olive oil
- 1 tablespoon Mexican oregano
- 2 tablespoons lime juice
- 1 teaspoon chili powder
- 1 teaspoon ground cumin
- Sea salt, to taste

1. Preheat the air fryer to 360ºF (182ºC). 2. In a bowl, toss the tortilla wedges with the remaining ingredients until evenly coated. Transfer the wedges to the crisper tray. 3. Insert the crisper tray into the air fryer, select the Air Fry setting, and cook the tortilla chips for about 5 minutes or until they are crispy, working in batches as needed. 4. Enjoy your homemade tortilla chips!

Honey Garlic Chicken Wings

Prep time: 5 minutes | Cook time: 18 minutes | Serves 4

- 2 pounds (907 g) chicken wings
- ¼ cup honey
- 2 tablespoons fish sauce
- 2 garlic cloves, crushed
- 1 teaspoon peeled and grated ginger
- 2 tablespoons butter, melted
- Sea salt and ground black pepper, to taste

1. Preheat the air fryer to 380ºF (193ºC). 2. In a bowl, toss the chicken wings with the remaining ingredients until well coated, then transfer them to the crisper tray. 3. Insert the crisper tray into the air fryer, select the Roast setting, and cook the chicken wings for 18 minutes, flipping them halfway through for even cooking.

Pecorino Cheese Stuffed Mushrooms

Prep time: 10 minutes | Cook time: 7 minutes | Serves 4

- 1 tablespoon butter
- 6 ounces (170 g) Pecorino Romano cheese, grated
- 2 tablespoons chopped chives
- 1 tablespoon minced garlic
- ½ teaspoon cayenne pepper
- Sea salt and ground black pepper, to taste
- 1 pound (454 g) button mushrooms, stems removed

1. Preheat the air fryer to 400ºF (205ºC). 2. In a mixing bowl, mix together the butter, cheese, chives, garlic, cayenne pepper, salt, and black pepper until well combined. 3. Fill each mushroom cap with the prepared filling, then arrange the stuffed mushrooms in the crisper tray. 4. Insert the crisper tray into the air fryer, select the Air Fry setting, and cook the mushrooms for about 7 minutes, shaking the tray halfway through for even cooking.

Crispy Beer-Battered Onion Rings

Prep time: 5 minutes | Cook time: 8 minutes | Serves 4

½ cup beer	
1 cup plain flour	pepper, to taste
1 teaspoon baking powder	2 eggs, whisked
1 teaspoon cayenne pepper	1 cup crushed tortilla chips
Sea salt and ground black	2 sweet onions

1. Preheat the air fryer to 380ºF (193ºC). 2. In a shallow bowl, combine the beer, flour, baking powder, cayenne pepper, salt, and black pepper. 3. In another shallow bowl, whisk the egg, and place the crushed tortilla chips in a separate bowl. 4. Dip each onion ring into the flour mixture, then into the egg, and finally coat with the tortilla chips. Arrange the coated onion rings in the crisper tray. 5. Insert the crisper tray into the air fryer, select the Air Fry setting, and cook the onion rings for about 8 minutes or until they are golden brown and cooked through.

Spicy Paprika Tortilla Chips

Prep time: 8 minutes | Cook time: 5 minutes | Serves 4

- 9 corn tortillas, cut into wedges
- 1 tablespoon olive oil
- 1 teaspoon hot paprika
- Sea salt and ground black pepper, to taste

1. Begin by preheating your air fryer to 360ºF (182ºC) to set the stage for cooking. 2. In a mixing bowl, toss the tortilla wedges with the remaining ingredients until they are well coated. Transfer the seasoned wedges to the crisper tray. 3. Insert the crisper tray into its designated position in the air fryer. Select the Air Fry setting and cook the tortilla chips for about 5 minutes or until they are crispy, shaking the tray halfway through. If necessary, work in batches to avoid overcrowding. 4. Once cooked, enjoy your delicious, homemade tortilla chips!

Savory Glazed Pork Ribs

Prep time: 5 minutes | Cook time: 35 minutes | Serves 4

- 2 pounds (907 g) spare ribs
- ¼ cup soy sauce
- ¼ cup rice vinegar
- ¼ cup sesame oil
- 2 garlic cloves, minced

1. Start by preheating the air fryer to 350ºF (180ºC). 2. Toss all ingredients in a lightly greased baking pan. 3. Place the baking pan in the corresponding position in the air fryer. Select Bake and cook the ribs for 35 minutes, turning them over halfway through the cooking time.

Spicy Chile Pork Ribs

Prep time: 5 minutes | Cook time: 35 minutes | Serves 4

- 1½ pounds (680 g) spare ribs
- Kosher salt and ground black pepper, to taste
- 2 teaspoons brown sugar
- 1 teaspoon paprika
- 1 teaspoon chile powder
- 1 teaspoon garlic powder

1. First, preheat your air fryer to 350ºF (180ºC) to prepare for cooking. 2. In a lightly greased crisper tray, toss all the ingredients together until well combined. 3. Insert the crisper tray into its designated position in the air fryer. Select the Air Fry setting and cook the pork ribs for 35 minutes, flipping them over halfway through to ensure even cooking. 4. Once finished, enjoy your tender and flavorful pork ribs!

Crispy Cheesy Broccoli Bites

Prep time: 5 minutes | Cook time: 10 minutes | Serves 4

- 1 pound (454 g) broccoli florets
- 1 teaspoon granulated garlic
- 1 tablespoon dried onion flakes
- 1 teaspoon crushed red pepper flakes
- 2 tablespoons olive oil
- ½ cup grated Pecorino Romano cheese

1. Preheat the air fryer to 370ºF (188ºC). 2. In a lightly oiled crisper tray, toss all the ingredients together until well combined. 3. Insert the crisper tray into the air fryer, select the Air Fry setting, and cook the broccoli florets for approximately 10 minutes, shaking the tray halfway through for even cooking. 4. Enjoy your meal!

Chapter 7

Vegetables and Sides

Chapter 7 Vegetables and Sides

Spiced Yukon Gold Air Fryer Potatoes

Prep time: 10 minutes | Cook time: 13 minutes | Serves 3

- ¾ pound (340 g) Yukon Gold potatoes, peeled and cut into 1-inch chunks
- 1 tablespoon olive oil
- Sea salt and ground black
- pepper, to taste
- ½ turmeric powder
- ½ teaspoon garlic powder
- ½ teaspoon paprika

1. First, preheat your air fryer to a hot 400ºF (205ºC) to prepare for cooking. 2. In a mixing bowl, toss the potatoes with the remaining ingredients until they are thoroughly coated on all sides. 3. Arrange the seasoned potatoes in a single layer in the crisper tray for even cooking. 4. Insert the crisper tray into its designated position in the air fryer. Select the Air Fry setting and cook the potatoes for approximately 13 minutes, shaking the crisper tray halfway through the cooking time to ensure they crisp up evenly. 5. Once cooked, enjoy your deliciously crispy potatoes!

Parmesan-Dill Air Fryer Broccoli

Prep time: 5 minutes | Cook time: 6 minutes | Serves 3

- ¾ pound (340 g) broccoli florets
- 1 tablespoon olive oil
- ½ teaspoon dried dill weed
- Coarse sea salt and freshly ground black pepper, to taste
- 2 ounces (57 g) Parmesan cheese, freshly grated

1. Start by preheating the air fryer to 395ºF (202ºC). 2. Toss the broccoli florets with the olive oil, dill, salt, and black pepper until well coated. 3. Arrange the broccoli florets in the crisper tray. 4. Place the crisper tray in the corresponding position in the air fryer. Select Air Fry and cook the broccoli florets for 6 minutes, shaking crisper tray halfway through the cooking time. 5. Top with the Parmesan cheese and serve warm.

Crispy Breaded Air Fryer Mushrooms

Prep time: 5 minutes | Cook time: 7 minutes | Serves 3

- ½ cup flour
- 2 eggs
- 1 cup seasoned bread crumbs
- 1 teaspoon smoked paprika
- Sea salt and ground black pepper, to taste
- ¾ pound (340 g) portobello mushrooms, sliced

1. Begin by preheating your air fryer to a sizzling 400ºF (205ºC) to prepare for cooking. 2. On a plate, spread out the flour. In a shallow bowl, whisk the eggs until well combined. In a third bowl, mix together the bread crumbs, paprika, salt, and black pepper to create the coating. 3. Dip each mushroom into the flour, ensuring it's fully coated. Next, dunk it in the whisked eggs, and finally toss it in the bread crumb mixture, making sure it's well coated on all sides. Arrange the coated mushrooms neatly in the crisper tray. 4. Insert the crisper tray into its designated position in the air fryer. Select the Air Fry setting and cook the mushrooms for about 7 minutes, turning them halfway through to achieve a golden, crispy exterior. 5. Once finished, enjoy your deliciously crispy mushrooms!

Garlic Butter Air Fryer Potatoes

Prep time: 5 minutes | Cook time: 18 minutes | Serves 3

- ¾ pound (340 g) potatoes, quartered
- 1 tablespoon butter, melted
- 1 teaspoon crushed garlic
- 1 teaspoon dried oregano
- Sea salt and ground black pepper, to taste

1. Start by preheating the air fryer to 400ºF (205ºC). 2. Toss the potatoes with the remaining ingredients until well coated on all sides. 3. Arrange the potatoes in the crisper tray. 4. Place the crisper tray in the corresponding position in the air fryer. Select Air Fry and cook the potatoes for about 18 minutes, shaking crisper tray halfway through the cooking time. 5. Serve warm and enjoy!

Spicy Chili Air Fryer Potatoes

Prep time: 10 minutes | Cook time: 13 minutes | Serves 4

1 pound (454 g) potatoes, diced into bite-sized chunks	Sea salt and ground black pepper, to taste
1 tablespoon olive oil	1 teaspoon chili powder

1. Start by preheating the air fryer to 400ºF (205ºC). 2. Toss the potatoes with the remaining ingredients until well coated on all sides. 3. Arrange the potatoes in the crisper tray. 4. Place the crisper tray in the corresponding position in the air fryer. Select Air Fry and cook the potatoes for about 13 minutes, shaking crisper tray halfway through the cooking time.

Spicy Air Fryer Sweet Potatoes with Salsa

Prep time: 5 minutes | Cook time: 35 minutes | Serves 4

1 pound (454 g) sweet potatoes, scrubbed and pricked with a fork	Coarse sea salt and ground black pepper, to taste
1 tablespoon olive oil	½ teaspoon cayenne pepper
	4 tablespoons salsa

1. Start by preheating the air fryer to 380ºF (193ºC). 2. Sprinkle the sweet potatoes with olive oil, salt, black pepper, and cayenne pepper. 3. Place the sweet potatoes in the crisper tray. 4. Place the crisper tray in the corresponding position in the air fryer. Select Air Fry and cook the sweet potatoes for 35 minutes, checking them halfway through the cooking time. 5. Split the tops open with a knife. Top each potato with salsa and serve.

Spicy Air Fryer Green Beans with Red Chile

Prep time: 5 minutes | Cook time: 8 minutes | Serves 3

¾ pound (340 g) fresh green beans, trimmed	1 teaspoon black mustard seeds
1 garlic clove, minced	1 dried red chile pepper, crushed
2 tablespoons olive oil	Sea salt and ground black pepper, to taste
1 tablespoon soy sauce	

1. First, preheat your air fryer to 380ºF (193ºC) to prepare for cooking. 2. In a mixing bowl, toss the green beans with the remaining ingredients until they are evenly coated. Arrange the seasoned green beans in a single layer in the crisper tray for optimal cooking. 3. Insert the crisper tray into its designated position in the air fryer. Select the Air Fry setting and cook the green beans for about 8 minutes, tossing the tray halfway through to ensure even cooking. 4. Once finished, enjoy your flavorful and perfectly cooked green beans!

Garlic Lemon Air Fryer Mushrooms

Prep time: 8 minutes | Cook time: 11 minutes | Serves 3

¾ pound (340 g) button mushrooms, cleaned and cut into halves	Sea salt and ground black pepper, to taste
2 tablespoons olive oil	1 tablespoon fresh lemon juice
1 garlic clove, pressed	1 tablespoon chopped fresh cilantro

1. Start by preheating the air fryer to 375ºF (190ºC). 2. Toss the mushrooms with the olive oil, garlic, salt, and black pepper. 3. Arrange them in a lightly oiled crisper tray. 4. Place the crisper tray in the corresponding position in the air fryer. Select Air Fry and cook the mushrooms for about 11 minutes, shaking crisper tray halfway through the cooking time. 5. Drizzle fresh lemon juice over the mushroom and serve with the fresh cilantro. Enjoy!

Herb-Infused Air Fryer Cauliflower

Prep time: 5 minutes | Cook time: 13 minutes | Serves 3

¾ pound (340 g) cauliflower florets	1 teaspoon dried basil
1 tablespoon olive oil	1 teaspoon dried rosemary
½ teaspoon dried oregano	Sea salt and ground black pepper, to taste

1. Begin by preheating your air fryer to a high 400ºF (205ºC) to prepare for cooking. 2. In a mixing bowl, toss the cauliflower florets and onion with olive oil and your choice of spices, ensuring they are well coated on all sides. 3. Arrange the seasoned cauliflower florets in a single layer in the crisper tray for even cooking. 4. Insert the crisper tray into its designated position in the air fryer. Select the Air Fry setting and cook the cauliflower florets for approximately 13 minutes, shaking the crisper tray halfway through the cooking time to ensure they crisp up evenly. 5. Once done, enjoy your deliciously roasted cauliflower florets!

Garlic Herb Air Fryer Fennel

Prep time: 10 minutes | Cook time: 15 minutes | Serves 4

1 pound (454 g) fennel bulbs, trimmed and sliced	1 teaspoon dried parsley flakes
2 tablespoons olive oil	Kosher salt and ground black pepper, to taste
1 teaspoon minced fresh garlic	

1. Start by preheating the air fryer to 370°F (188°C). 2. Toss all ingredients in a mixing bowl. Place the fennel in the crisper tray. 3. Place the crisper tray in the corresponding position in the air fryer. Select Air Fry and cook the fennel for about 15 minutes or until cooked through; check the fennel halfway through the cooking time.

Garlic Pecorino Chestnut Mushrooms

Prep time: 8 minutes | Cook time: 7 minutes | Serves 4

1 pound (454 g) chestnut mushrooms, quartered	Sea salt and ground black pepper, to taste
1 tablespoon olive oil	4 tablespoons shredded Pecorino Romano cheese
1 garlic clove, pressed	

1. Preheat the air fryer to 400°F (205°C). 2. In a bowl, toss the mushrooms with oil, garlic, salt, and black pepper until they are evenly coated on all sides. 3. Arrange the seasoned mushrooms in the crisper tray. 4. Insert the crisper tray into the air fryer, select the Air Fry setting, and cook the mushrooms for about 7 minutes, shaking the tray halfway through for even cooking. 5. After cooking, toss the mushrooms with cheese and serve immediately!

Cheesy Garlic Air Fryer Asparagus

Prep time: 5 minutes | Cook time: 6 minutes | Serves 4

1 pound (454 g) asparagus, trimmed	garlic
1 tablespoon sesame oil	Sea salt and cayenne pepper, to taste
½ teaspoon onion powder	½ cup Pecorino cheese, preferably freshly grated
½ teaspoon granulated	

1. Begin by preheating your air fryer to a hot 400°F (205°C) to prepare for cooking. 2. In a mixing bowl, toss the asparagus with sesame oil, onion powder, granulated garlic, salt, and cayenne pepper, ensuring they are evenly coated. Arrange the seasoned asparagus spears in a single layer in the crisper tray. 3. Insert the crisper tray into its designated position in the air fryer. Select the Air Fry setting and cook the asparagus for about 6 minutes, tossing them halfway through for even cooking. 4. Once cooked, sprinkle the asparagus with cheese for a delicious finishing touch. Enjoy your flavorful dish!

Spicy Air Fryer Bell Peppers

Prep time: 5 minutes | Cook time: 15 minutes | Serves 3

1 pound (454 g) bell peppers, seeded and halved	Kosher salt and ground black pepper, to taste
1 chili pepper, seeded	1 teaspoon granulated garlic
2 tablespoons olive oil	

1. Start by preheating the air fryer to 400°F (205°C). 2. Toss the peppers with the remaining ingredients; place them in the crisper tray. 3. Place the crisper tray in the corresponding position in the air fryer. Select Air Fry and cook the peppers for about 15 minutes, shaking crisper tray halfway through the cooking time. 4. Taste, adjust the seasonings and serve at room temperature.

Herb-Seasoned Air Fryer Italian Peppers

Prep time: 10 minutes | Cook time: 13 minutes | Serves 3

3 Italian peppers, seeded and halved	1 tablespoon chopped fresh parsley
1 tablespoon olive oil	1 tablespoon chopped fresh basil
Kosher salt and ground black pepper, to taste	1 tablespoon chopped fresh chives
1 teaspoon cayenne pepper	

1. Begin by preheating your air fryer to a sizzling 400°F (205°C) to prepare for cooking. 2. In a mixing bowl, toss the peppers with olive oil, salt, black pepper, and cayenne pepper until they are well coated. Place the seasoned peppers in the crisper tray. 3. Insert the crisper tray into its designated position in the air fryer. Select the Air Fry setting and cook the peppers for about 13 minutes, shaking the crisper tray halfway through to ensure even cooking. 4. After cooking, taste the peppers and adjust the seasonings as needed. Serve them warm, garnished with fresh herbs for an added burst of flavor!

Sesame Garlic Green Beans

Prep time: 5 minutes | Cook time: 7 minutes | Serves 4

1 pound (454 g) fresh green beans, trimmed	1 tablespoon soy sauce
1 tablespoon sesame oil	Sea salt and Szechuan pepper, to taste
½ teaspoon garlic powder	2 tablespoons lightly toasted sesame seeds

1. Preheat the air fryer to 380ºF (193ºC). 2. In a bowl, toss the green beans with sesame oil and garlic powder, then arrange them in the crisper tray. 3. Insert the crisper tray into the air fryer, select the Air Fry setting, and cook the green beans for 7 minutes, checking on them halfway through the cooking time. 4. After cooking, toss the green beans with the remaining ingredients and stir to combine thoroughly. Enjoy!

Buttery Dill Sweet Potatoes

Prep time: 10 minutes | Cook time: 15 minutes | Serves 2

2 sweet potatoes, peeled and halved	1 teaspoon dried dill weed
1 tablespoon butter, melted	Sea salt and red pepper flakes, to taste

1. Preheat the air fryer to 380ºF (193ºC). 2. In a bowl, toss the sweet potatoes with the remaining ingredients until evenly coated. 3. Arrange the seasoned sweet potatoes in the crisper tray. 4. Insert the crisper tray into the air fryer, select the Air Fry setting, and cook the sweet potatoes for 15 minutes, shaking the tray halfway through for even cooking. 5. Taste the sweet potatoes and adjust the seasonings as needed.

Egg-Stuffed Bell Pepper Cups

Prep time: 5 minutes | Cook time: 14 minutes | Serves 3

3 bell peppers, seeded and halved	3 tablespoons chopped green onion
1 tablespoon olive oil	Sea salt and ground black pepper, to taste
3 eggs	

1. Preheat the air fryer to 400ºF (205ºC). 2. In a bowl, toss the bell peppers with the oil, then place them in the crisper tray. 3. Crack an egg into each bell pepper half and sprinkle with salt and black pepper. 4. Insert the crisper tray into the air fryer, select the Air Fry setting, and cook the peppers for about 10 minutes. After that, top the peppers with green onions and continue cooking for an additional 4 minutes.

Spiced Garlic Green Beans

Prep time: 5 minutes | Cook time: 7 minutes | Serves 4

1 pound (454 g) fresh green beans, cleaned and trimmed	½ teaspoon dried dill weed
½ teaspoon garlic powder	1 teaspoon olive oil
½ teaspoon cumin powder	Sea salt and red pepper flakes, to taste
½ teaspoon onion powder	

1. Preheat the air fryer to 375ºF (190ºC). 2. In a bowl, toss the green beans with the remaining ingredients until they are evenly coated. 3. Arrange the coated green beans in the crisper tray. 4. Insert the crisper tray into the air fryer, select the Air Fry setting, and cook the green beans for 7 minutes, checking them halfway through for even cooking. 5. After cooking, taste the green beans, adjust the seasonings if necessary, and serve warm.

Paprika-Spiced Air Fryer Asparagus

Prep time: 5 minutes | Cook time: 6 minutes | Serves 3

¾ pound (340 g) fresh asparagus, trimmed	black pepper, to taste
Coarse sea salt and ground	1 teaspoon paprika
	2 tablespoons olive oil

1. Begin by preheating your air fryer to a high 400ºF (205ºC) to set the stage for cooking. 2. In a mixing bowl, toss the asparagus with salt, black pepper, paprika, and olive oil until they are well coated. Arrange the seasoned asparagus spears in a single layer in the crisper tray. 3. Insert the crisper tray into its designated position in the air fryer. Select the Air Fry setting and cook the asparagus for approximately 6 minutes, tossing them halfway through to ensure even cooking. 4. Once done, enjoy your perfectly crisp and flavorful asparagus!

Spicy Buttery Brussels Sprouts

Prep time: 5 minutes | Cook time: 10 minutes | Serves 3

- ¾ pound (340 g) Brussels sprouts, trimmed
- 1 tablespoon butter, melted
- 1 teaspoon crushed red pepper flakes
- Kosher salt and ground black pepper, to taste

1. Preheat the air fryer to 380ºF (193ºC). 2. In a bowl, toss the Brussels sprouts with butter and spices until they are evenly coated on all sides, then arrange them in the crisper tray. 3. Insert the crisper tray into the air fryer, select the Roast setting, and cook the Brussels sprouts for 10 minutes, shaking the tray halfway through for even cooking. 4. Serve warm and enjoy your dish!

Spiced Herb-Roasted Parsnips

Prep time: 5 minutes | Cook time: 10 minutes | Serves 4

- 1 pound (454 g) parsnips, trimmed
- 1 tablespoon olive oil
- 1 teaspoon herbes de Provence
- 1 teaspoon cayenne pepper
- Sea salt and ground black pepper, to taste

1. Preheat the air fryer to 380ºF (193ºC). 2. In a bowl, toss the parsnips with olive oil and spices until they are evenly coated on all sides, then arrange them in the crisper tray. 3. Insert the crisper tray into the air fryer, select the Air Fry setting, and cook the parsnips for 10 minutes, shaking the tray halfway through for even cooking.

Roasted Cauliflower and Onion

Prep time: 5 minutes | Cook time: 13 minutes | Serves 3

- ¾ pound (340 g) cauliflower florets
- 1 large onion, cut into wedges
- 2 cloves garlic, pressed
- 1 tablespoon olive oil
- Sea salt and ground black pepper, to taste
- 1 teaspoon paprika

1. Preheat the air fryer to 400ºF (205ºC). 2. In a bowl, toss the cauliflower florets and onion with garlic, olive oil, and spices until evenly coated on all sides. 3. Arrange the seasoned vegetables in the crisper tray. 4. Insert the crisper tray into the air fryer, select the Air Fry setting, and cook the vegetables for approximately 13 minutes, shaking the tray halfway through for even cooking.

Chapter
8

Vegetarian Mains

Chapter 8 Vegetarian Mains

Turmeric-Spiced Air Fryer Cauliflower

Prep time: 5 minutes | Cook time: 15 minutes | Serves 3

- 1 pound (454 g) cauliflower florets
- 2 teaspoons olive oil
- ½ teaspoon turmeric powder
- ½ teaspoon smoked paprika
- Sea salt and ground black pepper, to taste

1. Begin by preheating your air fryer to 350°F (180°C) to prepare for cooking. 2. In a mixing bowl, toss the cauliflower florets with the remaining ingredients until they are evenly coated. Transfer the seasoned florets to the crisper tray for cooking. 3. Insert the crisper tray into its designated position in the air fryer. Select the Air Fry setting and cook the cauliflower florets for approximately 15 minutes, turning them over halfway through to ensure even cooking. 4. Once cooked, enjoy your deliciously crispy cauliflower florets!

Spicy Vegan Mayo Air Fryer Parsnips

Prep time: 10 minutes | Cook time: 15 minutes | Serves 4

- 1 pound (454 g) parsnip, trimmed and sliced
- 2 tablespoons vegan mayonnaise
- ½ teaspoon cayenne pepper
- ½ teaspoon dried oregano
- Kosher salt and ground black pepper, to taste

1. Begin by preheating your air fryer to a hot 400°F (205°C) to get it ready for cooking. 2. In a mixing bowl, toss the parsnip slices with the remaining ingredients until they are well coated. Place the seasoned parsnips in the crisper tray. 3. Insert the crisper tray into its designated position in the air fryer. Select the Air Fry setting and cook the parsnip slices for about 15 minutes, shaking the crisper tray occasionally to ensure they cook evenly. 4. Once finished, serve warm and enjoy your deliciously roasted parsnips!

Spicy Garlic Air Fryer Cauliflower

Prep time: 5 minutes | Cook time: 15 minutes | Serves 4

- 1 pound (454 g) cauliflower florets
- 2 tablespoon olive oil
- 1 teaspoon minced garlic
- ½ teaspoon cayenne pepper
- Sea salt and ground black pepper, to taste

1. Start by preheating the air fryer to 350°F (180°C). 2. Toss the cauliflower florets with the remaining ingredients. Transfer to the crisper tray. 3. Place the crisper tray in the corresponding position in the air fryer. Select Air Fry and cook the cauliflower florets for about 15 minutes, tossing the crisper tray halfway through the cooking time.

Spiced Air Fryer Cauliflower Bites

Prep time: 5 minutes | Cook time: 15 minutes | Serves 4

- 1 pound (454 g) cauliflower florets
- Sea salt and ground black pepper, to taste
- 1 teaspoon ground ginger
- ¼ teaspoon ground cloves
- ½ teaspoon ground cumin
- ½ teaspoon coriander
- ½ teaspoon cayenne pepper
- 2 tablespoons olive oil
- 4 tablespoons cornflour

1. Begin by preheating your air fryer to 350°F (180°C) to prepare for cooking. 2. In a mixing bowl, toss the cauliflower florets with the remaining ingredients until they are evenly coated. Transfer the seasoned florets to the crisper tray. 3. Insert the crisper tray into its designated position in the air fryer. Select the Air Fry setting and cook the cauliflower florets for approximately 15 minutes, flipping them over halfway through to ensure they are cooked evenly. 4. Once done, enjoy your deliciously crispy cauliflower florets!

Garlic Mayo Air Fryer Green Beans

Prep time: 6 minutes | Cook time: 6 minutes | Serves 3

- ¾ pound (340 g) green beans, trimmed and halved
- ½ cup vegan mayonnaise
- 1 teaspoon granulated garlic
- 1 teaspoon paprika
- Kosher salt and ground black pepper, to taste

1. Start by preheating the air fryer to 390ºF (199ºC). 2. Toss the green beans with the remaining ingredients until well coated on all sides. Transfer to the crisper tray. 3. Place the crisper tray in the corresponding position in the air fryer. Select Air Fry and cook the green beans for about 6 minutes, tossing the crisper tray halfway through the cooking time. 4. Enjoy!

Herb-Crusted Air Fryer Potatoes with Thyme

Prep time: 5 minutes | Cook time: 20 minutes | Serves 3

- 1 pound (454 g) baby potatoes
- 2 tablespoons olive oil
- 1 teaspoon dried thyme
- 1 teaspoon dried rosemary
- 1 teaspoon dried basil
- 1 teaspoon dried oregano
- 1 teaspoon dried parsley flakes
- 1 teaspoon minced garlic
- Sea salt and ground black pepper, to taste
- 1 teaspoon cayenne pepper

1. Start by preheating the air fryer to 400ºF (205ºC). 2. Toss the potatoes with the remaining ingredients until well coated on all sides. 3. Arrange the potatoes in the crisper tray. 4. Place the crisper tray in the corresponding position in the air fryer. Select Air Fry and cook the potatoes for about 20 minutes, shaking the crisper tray halfway through the cooking time.

Herbed Air Fryer Polenta with Marinara

Prep time: 5 minutes | Cook time: 15 minutes | Serves 2

- ½ pound (227 g) polenta
- 2 tablespoons olive oil, plus more as needed
- 1 teaspoon dried basil
- 1 teaspoon dried oregano
- ¼ cup marinara sauce

1. Begin by preheating your air fryer to 350ºF (180ºC) to prepare for cooking. 2. Cut the polenta into bite-sized pieces and toss each piece with olive oil, basil, oregano, and marinara sauce until well coated. Transfer the seasoned polenta bites to the crisper tray. 3. Insert the crisper tray into its designated position in the air fryer. Select the Air Fry setting and cook the polenta bites for approximately 15 minutes, turning them over halfway through to ensure even cooking. 4. Once cooked, enjoy your deliciously crispy polenta bites!

Red Wine Marinated Air Fryer Tofu

Prep time: 8 minutes | Cook time: 22 minutes | Serves 4

- 14 ounces (397 g) extra-firm tofu, pressed and cubed
- 2 tablespoons soy sauce
- 1 tablespoon Dijon mustard
- ¼ cup red wine
- 2 teaspoons sesame oil
- 1 teaspoon minced garlic
- 1 chili pepper, seeded and minced
- 4 tablespoons corn flour
- Sea salt and ground black pepper, to taste

1. Toss the tofu with the soy sauce, mustard, red wine, sesame oil, garlic, and chili pepper. Let it marinate for 30 minutes. 2. Preheat the air fryer to 360ºF (182ºC). 3. Toss the tofu cubes with the corn flour, salt, and black pepper; place them in the crisper tray, discarding the marinade. 4. Place the crisper tray in the corresponding position in the air fryer. Select Air Fry and cook the tofu cubes for 10 minutes; shake the crisper tray and continue to cook for 12 minutes more.

Vegan Cheddar Stuffed Peppers

Prep time: 10 minutes | Cook time: 15 minutes | Serves 3

- 6 Italian peppers, seeded and stems removed
- 2 garlic cloves, minced
- 1 tablespoon taco seasoning mix
- ½ cup grated vegan Cheddar cheese
- Sea salt and red pepper flakes, to taste
- 2 tablespoons olive oil

1. Preheat the air fryer to 400ºF (205ºC). 2. Arrange the peppers in the crisper tray. 3. In a bowl, mix the remaining ingredients until well combined, then divide the filling among the peppers. 4. Insert the crisper tray into the air fryer, select the Air Fry setting, and cook the peppers for about 15 minutes.

Citrus Balsamic Roasted Beets

Prep time: 10 minutes | Cook time: 30 minutes | Serves 3

- 1 pound (454 g) beets, peeled and diced
- 2 tablespoons olive oil
- Sea salt and ground black pepper, to taste
- 1 tablespoon stone-ground
- mustard
- 2 tablespoons balsamic vinegar
- ¼ cup fresh orange juice
- 1 tablespoon chopped fresh rosemary

1. Preheat the air fryer to 390°F (199°C). 2. In a bowl, toss the red beets with the remaining ingredients until they are evenly coated on all sides, then transfer them to the crisper tray. 3. Insert the crisper tray into the air fryer, select the Air Fry setting, and cook the red beets for approximately 30 minutes, tossing the tray every 10 minutes for even cooking.

Tofu and Corn Stuffed Bell Peppers

Prep time: 6 minutes | Cook time: 15 minutes | Serves 2

- 2 bell peppers, seeded and halved
- 4 ounces (113 g) firm tofu, crumbled
- 4 tablespoons canned sweetcorn
- 1 tomato, crushed
- Sea salt and ground black pepper, to taste
- 1 teaspoon minced garlic
- 1 teaspoon smoked paprika

1. Preheat the air fryer to 400°F (205°C). 2. Arrange the peppers in the crisper tray. 3. In a bowl, mix the remaining ingredients until well combined, then divide the filling among the peppers. 4. Insert the crisper tray into the air fryer, select the Air Fry setting, and cook the peppers for about 15 minutes.

Smoky White Bean Sausages

Prep time: 5 minutes | Cook time: 15 minutes | Serves 3

- 1 cup canned white beans, drained and rinsed
- 1 medium onion, chopped
- 2 cloves garlic, chopped
- 2 tablespoons olive oil
- 1 teaspoon liquid smoke
- 2 tablespoons buckwheat flour

1. Preheat the air fryer to 390°F (199°C). 2. In a food processor, pulse all the ingredients until they are well incorporated. 3. Shape the mixture into three sausage links and place them in a lightly greased crisper tray. 4. Insert the crisper tray into the air fryer, select the Air Fry setting, and cook the sausages for about 15 minutes, shaking the tray halfway through for even cooking.

Herb Tomato Stuffed Eggplant

Prep time: 8 minutes | Cook time: 15 minutes | Serves 2

- 2 small eggplants, halved lengthwise
- 1 tablespoon olive oil
- 1 small shallot, chopped
- 2 garlic cloves, minced
- 1 bell pepper, chopped
- 1 medium tomato, chopped
- 2 tablespoons minced fresh parsley
- 1 tablespoon minced fresh basil
- Sea salt and ground black pepper, to taste

1. Preheat the air fryer to 400°F (205°C). 2. Toss the eggplants with the oil, then arrange them in the crisper tray. 3. In a bowl, mix the remaining ingredients to create the filling, and spoon it into the eggplant halves. 4. Insert the crisper tray into the air fryer, select the Air Fry setting, and cook the stuffed eggplants for about 15 minutes. 5. Serve warm and enjoy your dish!

Air Fryer Chickpea and Carrot Veggie Meatballs

Prep time: 12 minutes | Cook time: 15 minutes | Serves 4

- 16 ounces (454 g) canned chickpeas, rinsed and drained
- 1 medium onion, chopped
- 3 cloves garlic, roughly chopped
- 1 large carrot, peeled and roughly chopped
- ¼ cup roughly chopped fresh parsley
- ¼ cup roughly chopped fresh coriander
- ½ teaspoon peeled and grated ginger
- ½ teaspoon ground cinnamon
- 2 tablespoons olive oil
- Sea salt and ground black pepper, to taste

1. Start by preheating the air fryer to 380°F (193°C). 2. Pulse all the ingredients in the food processor until everything is well incorporated. 3. Form the mixture into balls and place them in a lightly greased crisper tray. 4. Place the crisper tray in the corresponding position in the air fryer. Select Air Fry and cook the meatballs for about 15 minutes, shaking the crisper tray occasionally to ensure even cooking. 5. Serve in pita bread with toppings of the choice. Enjoy!

Crispy Cornmeal-Coated Cucumbers

Prep time: 10 minutes | Cook time: 15 minutes | Serves 4

- 2 cucumbers, sliced
- 2 tablespoons olive oil
- ½ cup cornmeal
- Sea salt and ground black pepper, to taste

1. Preheat the air fryer to 400ºF (205ºC). 2. In a bowl, toss the cucumbers with the remaining ingredients until evenly coated, then place them in the crisper tray. 3. Insert the crisper tray into the air fryer, select the Air Fry setting, and cook the cucumbers for about 15 minutes, shaking the tray occasionally for even cooking. 4. Serve warm and enjoy your dish!

Spicy Cayenne Zucchini Crisps

Prep time: 8 minutes | Cook time: 10 minutes | Serves 4

- 1 pound (454 g) zucchini, sliced
- 1 tablespoon ground chia seeds
- ½ cup crushed crackers
- 2 tablespoons olive oil
- 1 teaspoon cayenne pepper
- Kosher salt and ground black pepper, to taste

1. Preheat the air fryer to 390ºF (199ºC). 2. In a bowl, mix the remaining ingredients to create the batter. Dip the zucchini slices into the batter, ensuring they are well coated, then arrange them in a single layer in the crisper tray. 3. Insert the crisper tray into the air fryer, select the Air Fry setting, and cook the zucchini slices for about 10 minutes, shaking the tray halfway through for even cooking. Repeat in batches as needed.

Herb-Roasted Potatoes with Tofu Cheese

Prep time: 10 minutes | Cook time: 20 minutes | Serves 3

- 1 pound (454 g) French fingerling potatoes, halved lengthwise
- 2 tablespoons olive oil
- 2 cloves garlic, pressed
- 1 tablespoon chopped fresh parsley
- 1 tablespoon chopped fresh coriander
- 1 tablespoon chopped fresh chives
- Sea salt and ground black pepper, to taste
- 2 ounces (57 g) tofu cheese, crumbled

1. Preheat the air fryer to 400ºF (205ºC). 2. In a bowl, toss the potatoes with all the remaining ingredients except for the tofu cheese until they are evenly coated on all sides. 3. Arrange the coated potatoes in the crisper tray. 4. Insert the crisper tray into the air fryer, select the Air Fry setting, and cook the potatoes for about 15 minutes, shaking the tray halfway through for even cooking. 5. After 15 minutes, top the potatoes with the tofu cheese and continue cooking for an additional 5 minutes.

Balsamic Glazed Air-Fried Red Beets

Prep time: 10 minutes | Cook time: 30 minutes | Serves 4

- 1 pound (454 g) red beets, peeled and diced
- 2 teaspoons olive oil
- Coarse sea salt and ground black pepper, to taste
- 2 tablespoons agave syrup
- 2 tablespoons balsamic vinegar

1. Preheat the air fryer to 390°F (199°C). 2. In a bowl, toss the red beets with the remaining ingredients until they are evenly coated on all sides, then transfer them to the crisper tray. 3. Insert the crisper tray into the air fryer, select the Air Fry setting, and cook the red beets for about 30 minutes, tossing the tray every 10 minutes to ensure even cooking.

Soy Glazed Cabbage Wedges

Prep time: 5 minutes | Cook time: 7 minutes | Serves 3

- 1 pound (454 g) Chinese cabbage, cut into wedges
- 2 tablespoons olive oil
- 2 tablespoons soy sauce
- 1 tablespoon rice vinegar
- 1 teaspoon stoneground mustard
- 1 teaspoon granulated garlic
- Sea salt and cayenne pepper, to taste

1. Preheat the air fryer to 350°F (180°C). 2. In a bowl, toss the cabbage wedges with the remaining ingredients until evenly coated, then transfer them to the crisper tray. 3. Insert the crisper tray into the air fryer, select the Air Fry setting, and cook the cabbage wedges for 7 minutes, shaking the tray halfway through for even cooking. 4. Taste the cabbage and adjust the seasonings as needed.

Lentil-Stuffed Air Fryer Eggplant

Prep time: 10 minutes | Cook time: 15 minutes | Serves 2

- 1 medium eggplant, halved
- 2 tablespoons olive oil
- 1 onion, minced
- 2 garlic cloves, minced
- 2 tablespoons tomato paste
- 6 ounces (170 g) canned red lentils, drained
- Sea salt and ground black pepper, to taste

1. Begin by preheating your air fryer to 400°F (205°C) to prepare for cooking. 2. Toss the eggplant halves with oil until they are well coated, then place them in the crisper tray. 3. In a separate bowl, mix the remaining ingredients to create the filling. Spoon the filling generously into each eggplant half. 4. Insert the crisper tray into its designated position in the air fryer. Select the Air Fry setting and cook the stuffed eggplants for about 15 minutes. Once cooked, serve warm and enjoy your delicious stuffed eggplants!

Chapter

9

Desserts

Chapter 9 Desserts

Cinnamon Plum Pie Cups

Prep time: 5 minutes | Cook time: 20 minutes | Serves 6

• 1 cup pitted and coarsely chopped purple plums	cinnamon
• ½ cup brown sugar	• 12 ounces (340 g) refrigerated flaky cinnamon rolls
• ½ teaspoon ground	

1. Begin by preheating your air fryer to 350ºF (180ºC) to set the stage for baking. 2. In a mixing bowl, toss the plums with sugar and cinnamon until they are evenly coated. 3. Spray the muffin cups with nonstick cooking spray to prevent sticking. Separate the dough into 6 rolls and gently press each roll into the prepared muffin cups. 4. Spoon the plum filling into each dough-lined cup, ensuring they are filled generously. Transfer the filled muffin cups to a baking pan for easy handling. 5. Insert the baking pan into the designated position in the air fryer. Select the Bake setting and cook the plum pie cups for about 20 minutes, or until the tops are golden brown. Enjoy your delightful plum pie cups once they're done!

Cinnamon Pear Pancake Bake

Prep time: 10 minutes | Cook time: 13 minutes | Serves 4

• 1 pear, peeled, cored, and sliced	• 2 tablespoons brown sugar
• 1 tablespoon lemon juice	• ½ teaspoon cinnamon
• 1 tablespoon coconut oil	• 2 eggs, whisked
• ½ cup all-purpose flour	• ½ cup milk
• ½ teaspoon baking powder	• ½ teaspoon vanilla extract

1. Begin by preheating your air fryer to 350ºF (180ºC) to prepare for baking. 2. Drizzle the pear slices with lemon juice and melted coconut oil, then arrange them evenly in the baking pan. 3. In a separate bowl, mix the remaining ingredients to create the batter. Pour the batter over the arranged pears, ensuring they are well covered. 4. Insert the baking pan into its designated position in the air fryer. Select the Bake setting and cook the pancake for about 13 minutes, or until it turns golden brown around the edges. Enjoy your delicious pear pancake once it's ready!

Spiced Butternut Squash Cakes

Prep time: 10 minutes | Cook time: 15 minutes | Serves 4

• 2 cups shredded butternut squash	• 1 tablespoon coconut oil
• ½ cup all-purpose flour	• 1 teaspoon pumpkin pie spice mix
• 2 eggs, beaten	

1. Preheat the air fryer to 360ºF (182ºC). 2. In a mixing bowl, combine all the ingredients thoroughly. 3. Spoon a portion of the batter onto the greased baking pan. 4. Insert the baking pan into the air fryer, select the Bake setting, and cook for 10 minutes, flipping the items halfway through for even cooking. 5. Repeat the process with the remaining batter and serve warm. Enjoy!

Coconut Cocoa Cake

Prep time: 5 minutes | Cook time: 20 minutes | Serves 6

• ½ cup coconut oil	powder
• 1 cup white granulated sugar	• ¼ teaspoon salt
• 2 eggs	• ¼ teaspoon grated nutmeg
• ½ cup all-purpose flour	• ½ teaspoon ground cinnamon
• ¼ cup coconut flour	• ¼ cup milk
• ½ teaspoon baking powder	• ½ teaspoon pure vanilla extract
• ½ cup unsweetened cocoa	

1. Preheat the air fryer to 340ºF (171ºC). 2. Lightly brush the sides and bottom of a baking pan with nonstick cooking spray. 3. In a mixing bowl, beat the coconut oil and sugar together until fluffy. Then, fold in the eggs and mix again until well combined. 4. Next, add the remaining ingredients and mix until everything is fully incorporated. Transfer the batter to the prepared baking pan. 5. Insert the baking pan into the air fryer, select the Bake setting, and cook for 20 minutes.

Coconut Blueberry Fritters

Prep time: 5 minutes | Cook time: 15 minutes | Serves 4

¾ cup all-purpose flour	A pinch of sea salt
1 teaspoon baking powder	1 egg
½ cup coconut milk	2 tablespoons melted butter
2 tablespoons coconut sugar	2 ounces (57 g) fresh blueberries

1. Start by preheating the air fryer to 360ºF (182ºC). 2. In a mixing bowl, thoroughly combine all the ingredients. 3. Drop a spoonful of batter onto the greased baking pan. 4. Place the baking pan in the corresponding position in the air fryer. Select Bake and cook for 10 minutes, flipping them halfway through the cooking time. 5. Repeat with the remaining batter and serve warm. Enjoy!

Air Fryer Raisin Butter Scones

Prep time: 5 minutes | Cook time: 17 minutes | Serves 5

1 cup all-purpose flour	A pinch of grated nutmeg
½ teaspoon baking powder	1 teaspoon lemon zest
½ cup granulated sugar	1 teaspoon vanilla extract
2 tablespoons raisins	¼ cup cold butter
A pinch of coarse sea salt	2 eggs, whisked

1. Start by preheating the air fryer to 360ºF (182ºC). 2. Mix all the ingredients until everything is well incorporated. Spoon the batter into baking cups; lower the cups into the baking pan. 3. Place the baking pan in the corresponding position in the air fryer. Select Bake and cook the scones for about 17 minutes or until a tester comes out dry and clean.

Cinnamon Egg Donuts

Prep time: 5 minutes | Cook time: 20 minutes | Serves 4

1 cup all-purpose flour	2 large eggs, whisked
½ teaspoon baking powder	2 tablespoons canola oil
¼ teaspoon sea salt	¼ cup milk
½ cup white sugar	½ teaspoon cinnamon powder

1. Begin by preheating your air fryer to 340ºF (171ºC) to prepare for baking. 2. In a mixing bowl, thoroughly combine all-purpose flour with baking powder, salt, and sugar until evenly mixed. 3. In a separate bowl, beat the eggs until frothy using a hand mixer. Add the oil and milk, beating again until well combined, then stir in the cinnamon powder and mix until everything is fully integrated. 4. Next, stir the egg mixture into the flour mixture, mixing gently until a dough ball forms. Be careful not to over-mix. Transfer the dough to a lightly floured surface. 5. Roll out the dough to a ¼-inch thickness using a rolling pin. Cut out doughnuts using a 3-inch round cutter, then use a 1-inch round cutter to remove the centers. Transfer the shaped doughnuts to the baking pan. 6. Insert the baking pan into the designated position in the air fryer. Select the Bake setting and cook for approximately 10 minutes, or until they are golden brown. Repeat the process with the remaining doughnut dough. Enjoy your freshly baked doughnuts!

Honey-Cinnamon Apricots with Mascarpone

Prep time: 10 minutes | Cook time: 16 minutes | Serves 4

8 apricots, halved and pitted	1 teaspoon ground cinnamon
1 tablespoon coconut oil, melted	2 ounces (57 g) mascarpone cheese
2 tablespoons honey	1 tablespoon coconut flakes

1. Preheat the air fryer to 340ºF (171ºC). 2. In a bowl, toss the apricots with coconut oil, honey, and cinnamon until well coated. 3. Arrange the coated apricots in a lightly oiled crisper tray. 4. Insert the crisper tray into the air fryer, select the Air Fry setting, and cook the apricots for 16 minutes. After cooking, top the fried apricots with mascarpone cheese and coconut flakes. Enjoy!

Apple Pie Danish Pastries

Prep time: 5 minutes | Cook time: 20 minutes | Serves 5

12 ounces (340 g) refrigerated puff pastry	1 cup apple pie filling

1. Preheat the air fryer to 350ºF (180ºC). 2. Roll out the puff pastry sheet into a large rectangle and cut it into triangles. 3. Spoon the filling into the center of each triangle, then fold the pastry over and seal the edges with your fingers. Transfer the filled pastries to the baking pan. 4. Insert the baking pan into the air fryer, select the Bake setting, and cook the Danish pastries for 20 minutes, or until the tops are golden brown.

Cocoa Spice Cupcakes

Prep time: 5 minutes | Cook time: 15 minutes | Serves 6

¾ cup all-purpose flour	¼ cup unsweetened cocoa powder
1 teaspoon baking powder	A pinch of sea salt
¼ teaspoon ground cinnamon	1 stick butter, room temperature
¼ teaspoon ground cardamom	¾ cup milk
¾ cup granulated sugar	2 eggs, beaten

1. Start by preheating the air fryer to 330ºF (166ºC). 2. Mix all the ingredients in a bowl. Scrape the batter into silicone baking molds; place them in the baking pan. 3. Place the baking pan in the corresponding position in the air fryer. Select Bake and cook the cupcakes for about 15 minutes or until a tester comes out dry and clean. 4. Allow the cupcakes to cool before unmolding and serving.

Vanilla Coconut Pancake Cups

Prep time: 5 minutes | Cook time: 5 minutes | Serves 4

½ cup flour	1 teaspoon vanilla paste
2 eggs	¼ teaspoon ground cinnamon
⅓ cup coconut milk	A pinch of ground cardamom
1 tablespoon coconut oil, melted	

1. Preheat the air fryer to 330ºF (166ºC). 2. In a mixing bowl, combine all the ingredients until well mixed. 3. Allow the batter to rest for 20 minutes, then spoon it into a greased muffin tin. Transfer the muffin tin to a baking pan. 4. Insert the baking pan into the air fryer, select the Bake setting, and cook for 4 to 5 minutes or until golden brown. Serve with your choice of toppings.

Cinnamon Apple Spice Cake

Prep time: 10 minutes | Cook time: 13 minutes | Serves 3

⅓ cup all-purpose flour	A pinch of kosher salt
¼ cup coconut flour	2 eggs, beaten
½ teaspoon baking powder	½ teaspoon pure vanilla extract
½ teaspoon ground cinnamon	¼ cup full-fat milk
3 tablespoons brown sugar	2 small apples, peeled, cored, and grated

1. Begin by preheating your air fryer to 350ºF (180ºC) to prepare for baking. 2. In a mixing bowl, combine all the ingredients thoroughly to create a smooth batter. Pour the batter into a lightly oiled baking pan, ensuring it's spread evenly. 3. Insert the baking pan into the designated position in the air fryer. Select the Bake setting and cook the cake for about 13 minutes, or until the edges are golden brown and a toothpick inserted into the center comes out clean. Enjoy your deliciously baked cake once it's ready!

Pumpkin Spice Honey Cake

Prep time: 5 minutes | Cook time: 13 minutes | Serves 3

4 tablespoons all-purpose flour	spice blend
	A pinch of Himalayan salt
4 tablespoons almond flour	¼ cup milk
1 teaspoon baking powder	¼ cup canned pumpkin
4 tablespoons honey	1 egg, beaten
1 teaspoon pumpkin pie	

1. Begin by preheating your air fryer to 350ºF (180ºC) to get ready for baking. 2. In a mixing bowl, combine all the ingredients to create a smooth batter. Pour the batter into a lightly oiled baking pan, ensuring it spreads evenly. 3. Insert the baking pan into its designated position in the air fryer. Select the Bake setting and cook the cake for about 13 minutes, or until the edges are golden brown and a toothpick inserted into the center comes out clean. Enjoy your delicious cake once it's done!

Cinnamon Pear Pancake

Prep time: 10 minutes | Cook time: 13 minutes | Serves 4

1 pear, peeled, cored, and sliced	2 tablespoons brown sugar
	½ teaspoon cinnamon
1 tablespoon lemon juice	2 eggs, whisked
1 tablespoon coconut oil	½ cup milk
½ cup all-purpose flour	½ teaspoon vanilla extract
½ teaspoon baking powder	

1. Preheat the air fryer to 350ºF (180ºC). 2. Drizzle the pear slices with lemon juice and melted coconut oil, then arrange them in the baking pan. 3. In a separate bowl, mix the remaining ingredients to create the batter, then pour it over the arranged pears. 4. Insert the baking pan into the air fryer, select the Bake setting, and cook the pancake for about 13 minutes, or until it is golden brown around the edges.

Coconut Cinnamon Plantain Boats

Prep time: 6 minutes | Cook time: 7 minutes | Serves 2

- 2 plantains, peeled
- ½ cup shredded coconut
- 1 tablespoon coconut oil
- 4 tablespoons brown sugar
- ½ teaspoon cinnamon powder
- ½ teaspoon cardamom powder
- 4 tablespoons raisins

1. Preheat the air fryer to 395ºF (202ºC). 2. Slice the plantains lengthwise while still in the peel, being careful not to cut all the way through. 3. Fill each plantain pocket with the remaining ingredients, dividing them evenly. 4. Arrange the filled plantains in a baking pan. 5. Insert the baking pan into the air fryer, select the Bake setting, and cook for 7 minutes. 6. Enjoy eating with a spoon!

Air Fryer Chocolate Glazed Eclairs

Prep time: 5 minutes | Cook time: 20 minutes | Serves 4

Choux Pastry:

- ¾ cup all-purpose flour
- ¼ cup almond milk
- ½ cup water
- 6 tablespoons butter, room temperature

Chocolate Glaze:

- ⅓ cup heavy whipping cream

- 1 teaspoon brown sugar
- ¼ teaspoon kosher salt
- ¼ teaspoon grated nutmeg
- 3 eggs

- 2 ounces (57 g) semi-sweet chocolate chips

1. Start by preheating the air fryer to 360ºF (182ºC). 2. In a mixing bowl, thoroughly combine all the ingredients for the pastry. Place the batter in a piping bag fitted with a large open star tip. 3. Pipe the eclairs into strips and lower them onto the greased baking pan. 4. Place the baking pan in the corresponding position in the air fryer. Select Bake and cook the eclairs for 10 minutes, flipping them halfway through the cooking time. 5. Repeat with the remaining batter. Place the eclairs in the refrigerator while making the chocolate glaze. 6. Heat the whipping cream in a microwave; add in the chocolate and whisk until smooth sauce forms. 7. Top the chilled eclairs with the chocolate glaze and let it sit for about 30 minutes before serving.

Air Fryer Cinnamon Apple Fritters

Prep time: 8 minutes | Cook time: 20 minutes | Serves 4

- 1 apple, peeled and grated
- ¼ cup coconut oil, melted
- ¾ cup all-purpose flour
- 1¼ teaspoons baking powder
- ¼ teaspoon ground cinnamon
- 1 egg
- ½ cup milk
- 2 tablespoons granulated sugar

1. Start by preheating the air fryer to 360ºF (182ºC). 2. In a mixing bowl, thoroughly combine all the ingredients. 3. Drop a spoonful of batter onto the greased baking pan. 4. Place the baking pan in the corresponding position in the air fryer. Select Bake and cook for 10 minutes, flipping them halfway through the cooking time. 5. Repeat with the remaining batter and serve warm. Enjoy!

Cranberry Chocolate Cupcakes

Prep time: 5 minutes | Cook time: 15 minutes | Serves 6

Cupcakes:
- ¾ cup self-raising flour
- ¾ cup caster sugar
- ¼ cup cocoa powder
- A pinch of sea salt
- A pinch of grated nutmeg

Frosting:
- ½ cup butter, room temperature
- 1 teaspoon vanilla extract

- 2 eggs, whisked
- ½ cup buttermilk
- ½ stick butter, melted
- 2 ounces (57 g) dried cranberries

- 3 ounces (85 g) chocolate chips, melted
- 4 tablespoons heavy whipping cream

1. Preheat the air fryer to 330ºF (166ºC). 2. In a mixing bowl, combine all the ingredients for the cupcakes until well mixed. Pour the batter into silicone baking molds and place them in a baking pan. 3. Insert the baking pan into the air fryer, select the Bake setting, and cook the cupcakes for about 15 minutes, or until a tester inserted in the center comes out dry and clean. 4. In a separate bowl, beat all the ingredients for the frosting using an electric mixer until smooth. Pipe the frosting onto the cooled cupcakes.

Cinnamon Vanilla French Toast Baguette

Prep time: 5 minutes | Cook time: 8 minutes | Serves 2

- 2 eggs
- 2 tablespoons coconut oil, melted
- ¼ cup milk
- ½ teaspoon vanilla extract

- ¼ teaspoon ground cinnamon
- ⅛ teaspoon ground nutmeg
- 4 thick slices baguette

1. Preheat the air fryer to 330ºF (166ºC). 2. In a mixing bowl, thoroughly combine the eggs, coconut oil, milk, vanilla, cinnamon, and nutmeg. 3. Dip each piece of bread into the egg mixture, ensuring they are well coated, and then place the slices in a lightly greased baking pan. 4. Insert the baking pan into the air fryer, select the Bake setting, and cook the bread slices for about 4 minutes. Afterward, flip the slices and cook for an additional 3 to 4 minutes. Enjoy!

Coconut Cocoa Butter Brownies

Prep time: 5 minutes | Cook time: 20 minutes | Serves 6

- 1 stick butter, melted
- 1 cup brown sugar
- 2 eggs
- ¾ cup all-purpose flour
- ½ teaspoon baking powder

- ¼ cup cocoa powder
- 2 tablespoons coconut oil
- 1 teaspoon coconut extract
- A pinch of sea salt

1. Preheat the air fryer to 340ºF (171ºC). 2. Lightly spritz the sides and bottom of a baking pan with nonstick cooking spray. 3. In a mixing bowl, beat the melted butter and sugar together until fluffy. Then, fold in the eggs and mix again until well combined. 4. Add the remaining ingredients to the bowl and mix until everything is thoroughly incorporated. Transfer the batter to the prepared baking pan. 5. Insert the baking pan into the air fryer, select the Bake setting, and cook for 20 minutes. Enjoy your delicious treat!

Appendix 1:
Air Fryer Cooking Chart

Beef

Item	Temp (°F)	Time (mins)	Item	Temp (°F)	Time (mins)
Beef Eye Round Roast (4 lbs.)	400 °F	45 to 55	Meatballs (1-inch)	370 °F	7
Burger Patty (4 oz.)	370 °F	16 to 20	Meatballs (3-inch)	380 °F	10
Filet Mignon (8 oz.)	400 °F	18	Ribeye, bone-in (1-inch, 8 oz)	400 °F	10 to 15
Flank Steak (1.5 lbs.)	400 °F	12	Sirloin steaks (1-inch, 12 oz)	400 °F	9 to 14
Flank Steak (2 lbs.)	400 °F	20 to 28			

Chicken

Item	Temp (°F)	Time (mins)	Item	Temp (°F)	Time (mins)
Breasts, bone in (1 ¼ lb.)	370 °F	25	Legs, bone-in (1 ¾ lb.)	380 °F	30
Breasts, boneless (4 oz)	380 °F	12	Thighs, boneless (1 ½ lb.)	380 °F	18 to 20
Drumsticks (2 ½ lb.)	370 °F	20	Wings (2 lb.)	400 °F	12
Game Hen (halved 2 lb.)	390 °F	20	Whole Chicken	360 °F	75
Thighs, bone-in (2 lb.)	380 °F	22	Tenders	360 °F	8 to 10

Pork & Lamb

Item	Temp (°F)	Time (mins)	Item	Temp (°F)	Time (mins)
Bacon (regular)	400 °F	5 to 7	Pork Tenderloin	370 °F	15
Bacon (thick cut)	400 °F	6 to 10	Sausages	380 °F	15
Pork Loin (2 lb.)	360 °F	55	Lamb Loin Chops (1-inch thick)	400 °F	8 to 12
Pork Chops, bone in (1-inch, 6.5 oz)	400 °F	12	Rack of Lamb (1.5 – 2 lb.)	380 °F	22

Fish & Seafood

Item	Temp (°F)	Time (mins)	Item	Temp (°F)	Time (mins)
Calamari (8 oz)	400 °F	4	Tuna Steak	400 °F	7 to 10
Fish Fillet (1-inch, 8 oz)	400 °F	10	Scallops	400 °F	5 to 7
Salmon, fillet (6 oz)	380 °F	12	Shrimp	400 °F	5
Swordfish steak	400 °F	10			

Vegetables					
INGREDIENT	AMOUNT	PREPARATION	OIL	TEMP	COOK TIME
Asparagus	2 bunches	Cut in half, trim stems	2 Tbsp	420°F	12-15 mins
Beets	1½ lbs	Peel, cut in ½-inch cubes	1Tbsp	390°F	28-30 mins
Bell peppers (for roasting)	4 peppers	Cut in quarters, remove seeds	1Tbsp	400°F	15-20 mins
Broccoli	1 large head	Cut in 1-2-inch florets	1Tbsp	400°F	15-20 mins
Brussels sprouts	1lb	Cut in half, remove stems	1Tbsp	425°F	15-20 mins
Carrots	1lb	Peel, cut in ¼-inch rounds	1 Tbsp	425°F	10-15 mins
Cauliflower	1 head	Cut in 1-2-inch florets	2 Tbsp	400°F	20-22 mins
Corn on the cob	7 ears	Whole ears, remove husks	1 Tbps	400°F	14-17 mins
Green beans	1 bag (12 oz)	Trim	1 Tbps	420°F	18-20 mins
Kale (for chips)	4 oz	Tear into pieces,remove stems	None	325°F	5-8 mins
Mushrooms	16 oz	Rinse, slice thinly	1 Tbps	390°F	25-30 mins
Potatoes, russet	1½ lbs	Cut in 1-inch wedges	1 Tbps	390°F	25-30 mins
Potatoes, russet	1lb	Hand-cut fries, soak 30 mins in cold water, then pat dry	½ -3 Tbps	400°F	25-28 mins
Potatoes, sweet	1lb	Hand-cut fries, soak 30 mins in cold water, then pat dry	1 Tbps	400°F	25-28 mins
Zucchini	1lb	Cut in eighths lengthwise, then cut in half	1 Tbps	400°F	15-20 mins

Appendix 2: Recipes Index

A

B

C

D

E

Made in the USA
Columbia, SC
17 December 2024

49776782R00046